Body Language

Master The Psychology and Techniques Behind How to Analyze People Instantly and Influencing Them Using Body Language, Subliminal Persuasion, NLP and Covert Manipulation

By

Ryan James

© Copyright 2018 by Ryan James

All rights reserved.

The following Book is reproduced below with the goal of providing information that is as accurate and as reliable as possible. Regardless, purchasing this Book can be seen as consent to the fact that both the publisher and the author of this book are in no way experts on the topics discussed within, and that any recommendations or suggestions made herein are for entertainment purposes only. Professionals should be consulted as needed before undertaking any of the action endorsed herein.

This declaration is deemed fair and valid by both the American Bar Association and the Committee of Publishers Association and is legally binding throughout the United States.

Furthermore, the transmission, duplication or reproduction of any of the following work, including precise information, will be considered an illegal act, irrespective whether it is done electronically or in print. The legality extends to creating a secondary or tertiary copy of the work or a recorded copy and is only allowed with express written consent of the Publisher. All additional rights are reserved.

The information in the following pages is broadly considered to be a truthful and accurate account of facts, and as such any inattention, use or misuse of the information in question by the reader will render any resulting actions solely under their purview. There are no scenarios in which the publisher or the original author of this work can be in any fashion deemed liable for any hardship or damages that may befall them after undertaking information described herein.

Additionally, the information found on the following pages is intended for informational purposes only and should thus be considered, universal. As befitting its nature, the information presented is without assurance regarding its continued validity or interim quality. Trademarks that mentioned are done without written consent and can in no way be considered an endorsement from the trademark holder.

Table of Contents

Book #1 - How to Analyze People: How to Read Anyone Instantly Using Body Language, Personality Types, and Human Psychology

Introduction 6

Chapter 1: The Personality Types 8

Chapter 2: How Each Personality Type Communicates... 13

Chapter 3: Techniques for Cold Reading People... 18

Chapter 4: Using Profiling Techniques to Analyze People.. 20

Chapter 5: Using Words to Read People.. 24

Chapter 6: Reading Body Language Cues and Changing your State of Mind........... 27

Conclusion 35

Book #2 - How to Analyze People: Mastery Edition - How to Master Reading Anyone Instantly Using Body Language, Human Psychology and Personality Types

Introduction: The Importance of Analyzing Others Instantly 38

Chapter 1: Identifying Personality Types.. 45

Chapter 2: The Principles of Perceptions 56

Chapter 3: Body Language Speaks Volumes... 61

Chapter 4: Interpreting and Responding to the Message 68

Chapter 5: Three Key Elements to Connectivity... 74

Chapter 6: The Beauty of Successfully Analyzing Others.. 78

Conclusion: Congratulations on Your Read 80

Book #3 - Manipulation: The Definitive Guide to Understanding Manipulation, MindControl and NLP

Introduction 82

Chapter 1: What is Manipulation and How does it Work?....................................... 84

Chapter 4: How to Recognize Negative Manipulation 98

Chapter 5: How to Avoid being Manipulated 102

Chapter 6: A Guide to Positive Manipulation (Persuasion) 108

Conclusion 115

Book #4 - Manipulation: How to Master Manipulation, Mind Control and NLP

Introduction 117

Chapter 1: Avoiding Manipulative Relationships 118

Chapter 2: Mastering Subtle Manipulation Tactics 121

Chapter 3: NLP Mastery & Everyday Applications 130

Chapter 4: Mind Control Maven 135

Chapter 5: Traits of Easily Manipulated People 141

Chapter 6: Where To Be On Guard 144

Conclusion 147

Book #5 - Manipulation: The Complete Step by Step Guide on Manipulation, Mind Control and NLP

Introduction 150

Chapter 1: Manipulating the Mind through NLP 151

Chapter 2: Step #1—Building Rapport vs. Fear 158

Chapter 3: Step #2—Defining Desired Outcomes 164

Chapter 4: Step #3—Considering the Consequences 171

Chapter 5: Step #4—Be the Solution to their Problem 176

Chapter 6: Step #5—Assuming Success 182

Conclusion 186

Thank you! 187

Book #1

How to Analyze People

How to Read Anyone Instantly Using Body Language, Personality Types and Human Psychology

Introduction

Nonverbal signals are a major part of the way we communicate with those around us. It's something that everyone is using in social situations, all of the time, whether they are conscious of it or not. However, the majority of people only have a basic, subconscious understanding of body language and the way it functions. Luckily, if this skill isn't something you can do naturally, or if you only want to improve your existing abilities, there is information you can study and internalize to become better in this area, starting today. There are many advantages to taking the time to do this.

- **Increased Confidence:** When you know how to read people accurately, there is far less confusion. You know what they're trying to say to you and thus know exactly how to respond. When you can accurately decipher what body language cues people are sending, or understand them on a deeper level due to personality type, you can also accurately adjust your nonverbal signals to be appropriate for the occasion, resulting in the best outcome possible.

- **Improved Relationships:** Relationships are tough, and this is because much of the time, we don't know how to accurately read each other. Not only will you be able to tell when someone is interested in you when it comes to dating, but you'll be able to understand your loved one on a deeper level if and when you get into a more serious relationship. All relationships require trust and open communication, and this becomes a whole lot easier when you can read each other in an accurate and reliable way, then respond in kind.

- **Increased Personal Safety:** Learning how to analyze people is not only beneficial for self-confidence, it can also mean the difference between protecting yourself from dangerous situations and being victimized. In chapter 4, we will explore the biases that hold people back from accurately reading people and spotting red flags that could save your life.

- **A Better Social Life:** People who are socially awkward or simply don't know how to react out of shyness, are usually this way because they haven't yet learned how to both send accurate nonverbal cues and read those of other people. Maybe you're the type who likes to keep a wide circle of various acquaintances, or maybe your interest lies more in forming fewer, but deeper, bonds with people. Whatever your intentions are, learning how to analyze people will help you achieve your social goals and send the right signals to other people.

- **More Professional Opportunities:** Something that goes hand in hand with learning how to analyze people is building rapport a lot more quickly, which opens up the door for better opportunities in terms of your job or career life. An interviewer is much likelier to choose the candidate who sends the right impression or who they feel good about, and you have a better chance of fitting this profile when you are educated in reading nonverbal cues and accurately judging or assessing the body language of others.

As you can see, there's nothing to lose and everything to gain with teaching yourself these valuable skills. In this book, you will learn which signals to watch for to tell you who a person really is on the inside, along with how to apply this information. Thank you for downloading this guide and I hope you learn something interesting from it!

Chapter 1: The Personality Types

In an attempt to understand people and better analyze them in an accurate way it helps to have a basic understanding of common personality traits. Have you ever wondered why certain people attract the same type of person over and over, or why certain types of people hold similar positions in the business world? The answer is quite simple, most of the things we or others do personally and professionally can be attributed to our unique personality type.

While there are many books out there that tackle this subject, delving into the multitude of personality types as well as their subtypes, we've taken this opportunity to narrow it down for you and make it easier for you to identify particular types and their characteristics. Following are four key personality types and how you can more quickly identify and relate to them.

The Leader
These are the people who love to be in charge. They don't usually have to search for the position of leadership because the task typically falls to them regardless of what group of people they might surround themselves with. Leaders have strong personalities and are rarely afraid to choose a challenging course for their teams. They have overpowering confidence that causes others to naturally follow their lead. Leaders are quick thinkers and tend to be energetic.

Leaders hold positions in business as presidents, executives, administrators, and supervisors. They tend to arm their vocabulary with strong words that convey power and authority. While they smile you can still see tension in their facial expressions, as they always appear to be serious people. Their body language usually sends the same message. While talking to groups they usually use their hands and pace the room they're presenting to.

Money and prestige are highly important to these personality types. They often prefer high-priced vehicles, big homes, lavish vacation spots and the trophy spouse. Because they are serious people and driven, family and relationships usually take a backseat to their professional lives.

The Fraternizer
The Fraternizer rarely meets a stranger. They are the social butterflies of the world today. Fraternizers hold a commanding presence in a room full of people and attention seems to flow toward them effortlessly. Their out-going personalities convey optimism and enthusiasm and

Fraternizers have little difficult saying what's on their mind as they enjoy engaging others in conversation.

Fraternizers enjoy looking their best and hold positions such event planners or venue coordinators, anything that deals with the public on a personal level. They like nothing more than fun in every aspect of their lives. They love to be around people and enjoy entertaining. You'll find that Fraternizers have a great sense of humor and are rarely seen without a smile and open arms that invite everyone to join the party.

This personality type favors fun above all else. Their drive and determination is fueled by excitement as well as adrenalin. Fraternizers are risk takers who seek adventure through travel, group gatherings and outdoor activities.

The Identifier
Providing a listening ear is what Identifiers do best. For them there is rarely anything more important than a relationship built on trust and in-depth discussions that promote nurturing and soul-searching. They tend to pose open questions instead of standard questions that can be answered with a simple "yes" or "no" response. Identifiers will think before they respond, evaluating feelings more than thoughts. While they are very likable, Identifiers tend to be socially timid so others will most likely need to initiate the conversation.

Because of their compassion and ability to empathize, Identifiers make great counselors, teachers, nurses and volunteers. Identifiers are known to use words that convey trust and comfort. They're always available to help and are great care-givers. The body language of the Identifier is usually relaxed and open allowing others to feel relaxed as well.

Identifiers value people and relationships above all else and have an innate ability to care for others, both emotionally and physically. They often put others first while their needs may go unmet due to lack of time or resources.

The Perceiver
Self-control and cautious behavior are the primary traits of Perceivers. Typically preferring analysis over emotion, they thrive on order and clarity in both conversation and relationships. It's not uncommon for this personality type to seem stand-offish to others, but once you get to know them you'll quickly realize how dependable they can be.

Perceivers primarily hold positions that encourage working in autonomous environments. Because they prefer analytical thinking their careers usually consist of engineering, technology, mathematics, and scientific fields. They often prefer conversations relating to educational topics focusing on theories and facts exploring various aspects of the subjects being discussed. Perceivers don't usually engage in topics associated with anything that is emotionally based. Perceivers usually appear serious or thoughtful and their body language is often viewed as closed, with folded arms and an a tense or stressed demeanor.

Because they prefer facts and numbers over personal relationships, Perceivers usually form relationships with like-minded individuals who understand their lack emotion and their need for stability and structure.

It is more common than not that people possess more than one of these four basic personality types. For instance it is not uncommon for Leaders to also carry traits of Fraternizers, Identifiers, or Perceivers. However, it is extremely rare to find a true Perceiver who holds personality traits of any type other than Leader, and it is equally as difficult to find true Fraternizers who hold personality traits of anyone other than Leaders. Following are some examples.

The Leader-Fraternizer

Leader-Fraternizers have incredible energy and can be highly successful. These personality types are what famous motivational speakers and entrepreneurs are made of. Imagine someone who can takes risks socially and physically while maintaining an open circle of friends and acquaintances. Leader-Fraternizers will have you fighting for their cause with them without hesitation, never questioning their vision or path.

They rarely see anything in the world as unobtainable and will go to great lengths to find success. With their ability to motivate those around them effortlessly, Leader-Fraternizers are able to delegate quickly and without much deliberation. They're tuned-in to the people they are surrounded by and utilize this to their advantage never forgetting to repay their efforts with praise and encouragement.

The Leader-Identifier

Leader-Identifiers are less common and more subdued. While they are still successful they are not as likely to standout as the Leader-Fraternizers do. Leader-Identifiers make fantastic mentors and friends. They are well equipped mentally and emotionally to help you succeed while fulfilling their own agenda. Many of the traits of the Leader follow the Leader-Identifier, but you'll find that the Identifier quality causes them to be more approachable and their reasoning better understood.

The Leader-Identifier will also pay closer attention to the people they lead on a professional as well as personal level. These individuals basically have the best of both worlds with regard to personality make-up. They can be highly successful individuals and are able to adapt quickly to just about any environment because of their ability to read people and situations quickly.

While they are less apt to take the same risks as other personality types, the Leader-Identifier is able to meet the professional terms of a business as well as adapting to the rapport building skills of the Identifier alone. Many businesses search for these individuals to take positions as HR directors or marketing reps.

The Leader-Perceiver
While Leader-Perceivers are successful they are more difficult to get to know on a personal level. They prefer to keep subjects on target and leave little room for building a rapport based on any type of emotional bond. Leader-Perceivers are strong business figures with a great capacity for maintaining a path to specific goals, making sure nothing interrupts or interferes with the overall outcome of their agenda.

Because of their preference for working autonomously they are better suited for careers in areas related to technology or science simply because these areas focus less on emotion and more on facts or data.

The personal relationships of Leader-Perceivers are much like those of the Perceiver; they gravitate toward like-minded individuals preferring to keep emotion out of the equation as much as possible. This is not to say that this personality is not capable of emotion, it's just not something that is natural or extremely comfortable to them.

You're less likely to experience confrontation with this personality type. They are very good at assessing and categorizing their thoughts and/or feelings prior to any professional encounter and rarely react to situations without careful consideration.

The Fraternizer-Identifier
While it is rare, this combination does exist and they can be the most accepting, inviting people you'll ever encounter. The Fraternizer-Identifier might have a decreased energy level as

compared to the Leader-Fraternizer or the sole Fraternizer, but that is compensated by their ability to spread their positive outlook to others.

Fraternizer-Identifiers make an excellent youth counselor or life coach because of their ability to remain cheerful and emotionally grounded simultaneously. They are positive-thinkers and dislike conflict. It is likely that this personality type would be able to easily blend into most professional and social atmospheres with little difficulty.

While it may be hard to pin point the two personality traits at first, practice will enable you to identify them more quickly. Begin by looking first at the most obvious characteristics of the individual and go from there. Identifying key attributes such as the stress level in their facial expressions, body language, or how they speak with others, i.e. using "I" statements or inviting the other person into the conversation as a valuable participant can be important indicators of which defined personality they most likely adhere to. It will always be easier to identify the strongest characteristics first.

When all else fails trust your gut. We were all designed with an internal gauge that helps us to identify those around us and how we should relate to them. Look for that instinct and build upon it. Ask yourself how this person makes you feel; what it is about the person that makes you feel comfortable or uneasy depending on the circumstances? Would you feel comfortable with this person in a one-on-one conversation or are you more comfortable observing them from a distance. The better you know yourself the better you can identify and analyze others instantly.

Chapter 2: How Each Personality Type Communicates

As soon as you figure out which personality type someone fits into based on the information in the last chapter, you can figure out other aspects of their personality. Communication is the most important consideration in many respects, including relationships, social life, and more. You can use the following information to understand those around you based on this.

The first foundational quality of a person you should look for is whether they are emotionally-based or not. Fraternizers and Identifiers are typically emotionally based, while Leaders and Perceivers are not. The amount of emotion you can look for in a Leader or Perceiver depends on the other personality traits he or she maintains. We've provided examples below.

Leader-Fraternizer
You'll have a great time communicating with this personality type. They stay focused but are able to exert a great sense of humor and a fun while they're headed in the direction of their goal. Caution should be used in confusing this personality type with the solid Fraternizer type. Leader-Fraternizers are less "stuffy" as the typical Leader, but they are still quite goal oriented, so don't let that take a back seat to the humor and fun that can be experienced. Stay focused or they may quickly let you know your place. They don't like wasting time but they do enjoy a happy work-place.

Leader-Identifier
The Leader-Identifier is not as gregarious as the Leader-Fraternizer, but they are a calming influence if you're prone to anxiety or don't do well under pressure. These personalities, while extremely focused and professional will take the time necessary to incorporate emotional needs in your day-to-day interactions. It is important to remember that while they value you emotionally, your emotions should not get in the way of goal-oriented tasks. Leader-Identifiers are more likely to put themselves in your position, so to speak, before expecting more from you than you can provide. They understand where you're coming from. They want you to feel comfortable in your environment and usually maintain an open-door policy to help alleviate any miscommunication within the business setting.

Leader-Perceiver

The personality traits of the Leader-Perceiver closely match the traits of the Leader alone. They maintain a serious persona and you might find yourself wondering if you're able to maintain a strong working-relationship with this person. The key is to keep your communication on a business level, discussing things that pertain to achieving the tasks at hand. Your attempts to bring humor or emotion into your conversation or agenda will fall short of meeting their expectations. They prefer to remain on-task, and not waste precious time with such frivolity.

While this might make it simpler for some, chances are if you are an emotionally-based person, such as the Fraternizer or Identifier, it will be difficult for you to function effectively under the guide of the Leader-Perceiver. Generally speaking, emotion-based personalities require more communication than the Leader-Perceiver is able to give. But if you want something done efficiently and correctly with little interruption or interaction, these would be the people for the job.

Fraternizer-Identifier

The Fraternizer-Identifier communication style is probably the easiest and most rewarding. This person can be both fun and easy to build a strong rapport with. The Fraternizer-Identifier will take the time to communicate their feelings as well as encouraging and validating your feelings on a continuous basis. While they have a lot of energy they are more subdued than the person who carries only the traits of the Fraternizer.

Why is this information relevant and useful when it comes to analyzing or reading people? There are many different reasons why this is the case, but let's take the example of a professional situation. Before you enter a negotiation with someone else, knowing what type of personality traits they possess presents you with a distinct advantage. If you're a sales person, you will benefit more from noticing that your customer is a Perceiver and needs some time to reflect and think about the sale. Pressuring them will have a detrimental effect on their choice and lead them to say "no" when they might not have otherwise.

Successful relationships, both personal and professional, require effective communication. With a wide array of personalities we have a variance just as broad with communication types. The thing to remember, in all types of communication, is to think before you speak. How many times have you left a conversation wishing you had or had not said something in particular whether it was because it could be misconstrued or because it gave a false impression of who you truly are? If we're honest, we each have a story or two to share.

Even if you're a Perceiver by nature, there will be times that you will have to communicate. Each of us, regardless of our personality type, need to be familiar with how other prefer to communicate. It's not only a sign of respect it will leave a good impression if one of these types happens to be interviewing you for a position.

Now we'll take some time to go over each personality type and how they deal with personal communication.

Leader

Leaders are very direct and typically only use emotion when it will further their agenda or meet their goal. This is not to say that they are narcissistic in nature, it is simply not in their nature to incorporate emotion with their personal communication. Leaders have a difficult time separating business from pleasure. Leaders are often misconstrued as being cold or detached, when in fact they are trying to get things done in a constructive and productive manner. You can however teach a Leader to reach some level of feeling emotion by allowing them to take their time and learn from your ability to express your feelings. If you are truly an emotionally-based personality this relationship will take a lot of time and patience on your part.

Fraternizer

Fraternizers are a lot of fun but you might have a difficult time getting them to slow down and smell the roses. Because personal communication requires some degree of seriousness the Fraternizer may find it difficult to slow down long enough for something as mundane as serious chatter. It's not to say that the Fraternizer doesn't value personal relationships that might require more serious communication, it's that they are generally so free-spirited that they don't see the need to make everything so serious. The best plan of action is to incorporate your communication in a less serious tone. You can keep the communication style light and still convey the degree of intimacy that you may need.

Identifier

The Identifier will make personal communication easy, unless you're a Leader or Perceiver. Being emotionally-based people by nature they have no difficulty understanding what their ideas, feelings, and plans consist of and giving you ample opportunity to communicate your feelings as well. Identifiers are generally able to get along with just about anyone, because they are good at reading the body language and verbal cues of others. Their communication style is gentle in its approach and Identifiers are rarely confrontational. They generally think before they speak and are patient enough to allow you to do the same.

Perceiver

Personal communication with the Perceiver type personality can be tricky. Because they qualify information in an analytical frame of reference your communication skills will need to focus on that quality. You'll need to qualify the information you want to communicate in analytical terms before proceeding. For example, if you want to communicate to your Perceiver friend that you value your friendship, you'll need to phrase the information in this manner, "I feel as though I learn a great deal from you. I appreciate the time we spend discussing..." As long as you incorporate an analytical approach or an approach that can be measured in terms of growth, you'll be able to get your point across.

Leader-Fraternizer

The Leader-Fraternizer doesn't make personal communication very difficult, but you need to remember that they prefer direct statements presented in a light manner. It is best to stay away from communication techniques that incorporate vague feelings or a melancholy attitude. They take communication seriously and prefer presenting ideas instead of problems. Problems denote a need for immediate action while ideas allow them to weigh the outcome and calculate their approach from that aspect. The Fraternizer aspect of this personality allows the Leader to be more "in-tune" with their ability to communicate on a more personal level rather than dictating their expectations to the other party.

Leader-Identifier

Communicating with the Leader-Identifier is very easy to master. They don't shy away from in-depth discussion pertaining to personal relationships. They do, however, prefer to listen and act over listen and present. For example, if you tell a Leader-Identifier that you require more one-on-one attention, they will process the information and attempt to meet your need in their time frame. The results will not likely be instantaneous and they will probably ask for additional information to consider during the process, such as "why", "what" or "how".

Leader-Perceiver

The Leader-Perceiver communication style is factually based and doesn't leave room for emotionally charged discussions. Your personal communication with this individual is simple because there's little room for anything other than factual statements regarding expectation and how it will positively impact the relationship you share.

Fraternizer-Identifier

Communication on a personal level with a Fraternizer-Identifier type personality is light and easy. They prefer information of a personal nature to be presented in a light-hearted manner. They are open to hearing what you have to say and will respond likewise. While they typically don't prefer personal communication that includes long discussions that dwell on the emotional needs of the relationship, they do invite your opinions and thoughts openly.

Becoming more familiar with personal communication techniques is as easy as looking at your established relationships and how communication flows with regard to the other person and their particular type of personality. Remember to take into consideration your individual personality type because you in turn affect how others perceive and communicate with you. You may surprise yourself and hone the ability to expand on the positive attributes of your own personality and how you relate in both social and business situations.

Chapter 3: Techniques for Cold Reading People

Cold reading is an irreplaceable skill for anyone who wishes to master reading body language or analyzing people in general. This chapter will cover a few methods for doing that, but similar to any other skill, it does take plenty of practice to master it. Although it is typically associated with psychics, it's a logical process and works by selecting the language you use carefully and paying close attention to the responses of those you are attempting to read.

The our first method "Quick Statements", also referred to as "Shotgun Statements", is typically used by psychics or mediums generally always before other methods of cold reading are explored. This method uses as much information as possible with the idea that at least one thing you say should cause a reaction in the person. The purpose of this technique is being as vague as you can, allowing you to get a reaction from the individual or one of the individuals in the audience. This can't sound overly vague since most people would notice what you were doing, if it did. For example, if you're in a group of people you can mention slightly specific things such as "Very shy people usually do this," and see if it gets a reaction from anyone in the group.

When talking to someone on an individual level you can simply listen to what they say and try to make accurate guesses about the type of person they are. If they say, for instance, that they are usually very calm, you can use this information to make more accurate judgments about their current mood.

The Barnum Effect is the phenomenon where someone reads or hears something very general but believes that it applies to them. These statements appear to be very personal on the surface but in fact, they are true for many. Human psychology allows us to want to believe things that we can identify with on a personal level and even seek information where it doesn't necessarily exist, filling in the blanks with our imagination for the rest. This is the principle that horoscopes rely on, offering data that appears to be personal but probably makes sense to countless people. Since the people reading them want to believe the information so badly, they will search for meaning in their lives that make it true.

This provides you with a general area of information about someone that you can use to delve deeper and acquire more accurate, drilled-down answers from them. For example, you could say to someone, "It seems as though you've gone through a major change within the last year or so," and appear as though you know something specific about them, when this could apply to most people. They will often be surprised that you could tell this information and then proceed to fill in the blanks on their own.

You can give an accurate cold reading for someone by using information that was already given to or confirmed by you earlier in the conversation, this is referred to as reusing or recapping. Many therapists use this technique to begin building a quick rapport with their clients. As soon as you begin talking to them and using general Barnum statements, pay attention to how they respond. If they give specific details to you, save that information for later on in the conversation.

Although you won't always be in control of this aspect while trying to analyze or read people, it helps to find the right subject when possible. Choosing the correct person to observe makes a difference because some people are easier to read than others. When it comes to using cold reading to analyze people, you want someone who is open enough to finish your ideas and fill in the blanks with information about their self on a personal level. People who are very closed off or skeptical will make this much more difficult.

As soon as you have "warmed up" the person you are attempting to analyze or read by getting some predictions right, they are probably quite convinced at how perceptive you are by this point. This will lead them to loosen up or reveal more information with their nonverbal body signals, giving you another advantage that makes them easier to read. The idea is not to become a fortune teller or palm reader, but to draw off of those techniques to get better at analyzing people. This technique, in combination with the methods you will be given in the following chapters of this book, will make you a master at analyzing people.

Chapter 4: Using Profiling Techniques to Analyze People

What would you think of someone in your neighborhood that has children, goes out to work in a suit every day, has a clean house and great lawn, acts polite and friendly, seems to care about your day and life, and clears the snow from your driveway when you're away? The majority of people would assume that this person is great and genuine. So it might surprise you that someone who fit this description actually tortured people in his backyard. His name is David Parker Ray, a park ranger who appeared to admire and respect women but actually had been sadistically mistreating them for years. His neighbors were shocked and assumed that he was a regular guy, a nice guy.

This happens more than you realize, the assumption that people are okay just because they do the things that society expects of them. The problem is that even the most notorious criminals know how to appear as trustworthy or normal. If you watch or read the news, you rarely ever hear someone say, "Yeah, I thought he was up to no good." On the contrary, we hear over and over again how nice or normal or helpful someone was and how others can't believe that this same person could do such horrific things. Many times it's our own stereotypes that cause us not to delve deeper to see what's behind the curtain, or normal face.

We as society have grown complacent in accepting "nice" and "normal" appearances at face value and not looking any deeper thereby giving us a false interpretation of the individual we're looking at. If Mr. Ray's neighbors had looked more closely at him as opposed to his façade, they may have been able to identify key indicators that everything was not necessarily as it appeared. Because he is most likely narcissistic he would have given subtle clues to his true character. For example narcissists always have an ulterior motive for doing "nice" things. They don't do "nice" things when others aren't watching. They go out of their way to appear normal. Maybe if they had looked more closely to how Mr. Ray's family acted around him they would have seen another picture as well. Do others appear anxious around this individual or do they seem to go above and beyond to please the narcissist? Just because things appear okay on the outside does not mean that things are okay on the inside. The neighbors may not have seen Mrs. Ray out often or noticed the children out often. Narcissist's themselves are very good at controlling the individuals in their lives in hopes of controlling their overall appearance to others.

You might be asking yourself if it's possible to actually use profiling techniques to analyze anyone including the dangerous types of people as described above. The truth is a resounding "Yes!" It does, however, take practice and knowledge of what you should be looking for in terms of key factors used in this methodology. While there are many types of profiling techniques from a range of authorities such as law enforcement and the FBI, we are going to focus on those techniques most commonly used by professionals within behavioral medicine practices.

While someone could initially appear sincere or "normal", there are things you need to look at before making this conclusion too quickly:

Is their body language open or closed? People who are emotionally guarded tend to maintain a physical stance that suggests the same feeling. These types of people generally stand with their arms folded or their hands in their pockets. You can also tell quite a lot about a person when shaking their hand. If the hand is a firm grasp but pulls away quickly that could be a sign of being emotionally guarded or a lack of desire for truly opening up to the other individual. A firm handshake that lasts several seconds is adequate and should tell you that the person is open to knowing you. This feeling should be even further acknowledged if the person covers your shaking hand with their spare hand. Many people study handshakes and have the ability to convey a read that isn't necessarily accurate. For instance, sales people and politicians are keen at the hearty handshake, so it's very important to look at other indicators as well.

Do they have good eye contact? Those who are confident and typically honest will have appropriate eye contact. Eye contact is make-and-break over and over during an interaction. Someone who seems to stare right through you should not be trusted immediately. These types of individuals lack the ability to gauge natural eye contact and have most likely had to practice this to at least appear normal. They can also be very intimidating if they are doing this on purpose. On the opposite side, someone who is unable to maintain several seconds of direct eye contact without appearing uncomfortable could be either extremely shy or nervous.

What is their anxiety level portraying? People who are nervous or untrusting of their immediate surroundings are more apt to shift their weight back and forth and sometimes twist back and forth with their upper torso. Don't expect to see an obvious shift in body mechanics, this can be very subtle and the less the person desires to be seen for who they really are the more subtle the apparent anxiety will be to onlookers. You need to watch for several minutes before you can make your best assumption.

How do they look? This is a big one. And in today's society this can be a very touchy subject. We're not talking about judging someone based on their appearance, we are talking about how this person presents themselves to others. Let's look at couple of examples, because this can be complicated.

You are at a neighborhood barbeque and everyone is dressed in shorts, t-shirts, and tennis shoes. As you look around, you spot a male who is in slacks, a dress shirt and nicer shoes. This individual could have stopped in before going home to change or this could be someone who is unable to blend comfortably with others. If you're at a business-casual dinner party and someone is wearing a tie and dinner jacket or very expensive dinner dress, this person may be trying to appear more professional or more trustworthy. And then there is the offset that either of these people may take themselves too seriously.

Let's take a look at the above two scenarios and include body language and anxiety level. The nicely dressed individual at the pool party has their arms crossed and has their eyes darting back and forth between several people within the conversation. This person can be said to not only be uncomfortable with their environment but with themselves as well. If the person is perspiring, and the temperature isn't really a factor, you can be assured that this individual is ridden with anxiety and it's most likely not just shyness. Shy people are more able to blend in with their clothing choices and body mechanics. With the only identifying factors that separate anxiety from a threatening personality type being those of eye contact and anxiety level it is important to also view how others seem to respond to the individual's presence. Do others seem comfortable around this person? If so, the individual may very well be shy. But if others appear "put-off" or irritated by the individual you could be looking at a very different type of personality. Initially the practiced narcissist can appear as relaxed and inviting. But take a closer look. Try to observe them when others are not in their close proximity. Narcissists need "breaks" to refuel or reassess their environment. If you notice someone quite out-going who later steps back and begins searching the crowd, chances are that individual is reassessing their environment and fueling up for another go around.

When reviewing this information it's important to remember these things in using profiling techniques in analyzing people:

- What type of situation are you viewing the subject in?
- Is their personal appearance unkempt or is it activity appropriate?

- Does their body language suggest openness or the opposite?
- Are they using appropriate eye contact?
- What does their anxiety level suggest?
- How does this person seem to make those around them feel?

The more frequently you use these tools in analyzing others the easier it will be to formulate appropriate profiles of these individuals.

Chapter 5: Using Words to Read People

It is possible to get very accurate ideas about who someone is by closely listening to the words they choose to use in conversation. Listening to the clues a person gives while they speak presents you, the analyzer, with the perfect technique for reading them. Words are the way that we share and represent our thoughts, ideas, and moods. We can't ever be inside someone else's mind, but the closest we can ever be to understanding someone else is by listening to, or in some cases reading, their words.

Some words show behavioral traits in the person speaking or writing them, and provide us with clues to their personality. These clues increase the likelihood of predicting someone's behavior by thinking about which words they select when speaking or writing. They aren't enough, on their own, to determine someone's qualities or traits. However, they can give us valuable insights into how their thought processes typically function.

Begin by building your hypotheses. You can then extend your hypotheses based on additional clues and test them out by using further observations. You can then draw conclusions about that person based on credible information that you've gathered. Our brains are highly efficient machines, using nouns, verbs, adverbs, and adjectives to translate thoughts into language. We have choices that are practically endless in with regard to how we construct our sentences, and the words we do choose tell a lot about our thoughts and who we are as people.

An average sentence will contain a main subject along with a verb. The sentence, for instance, "I drove" contains the subject, "I" and the verb, "drove" which explains the action of the subject. When you add any extra information onto this simple sentence, you are shifting or modifying the meaning of the sentence. Looking at these modifications can give us clues as to the person behind the words. Paying attention to this can help you to develop a theory or hypothesis about the speaker and figure out who they are on a deeper level.

For example, if you are talking to another person and they dominate the conversation with the word "I" or "my" you can easily assume that they are self-absorbed. This assumption is based on their need to "own" the conversation. Typically the only instances this person will use an alternative word choice is when they are assigning unwanted responsibility to another person. There are varying degrees of self-absorption that can indicate what level of sociopathy they might carry. Those with a high level of sociopathy or narcissism will have firm, strong language skills that are quite capable of steering a complete conversation with another person. The narcissist has had years of practice in speaking in a way that others will respond to in a manner that is acceptable and predictable by the narcissist.

Someone else who uses the "I" or "my" quite often but isn't very high on the level of sociopathy is someone who has a lower self-esteem but want to present themselves in a different light. They desire and need to be seen as strong and competent but don't usually have the necessary social skills to adequately portray this mindset. Another easy way to differentiate between these two types is how they present themselves. The first individual uses firm, strong language while the second individual will seem almost as if they are asking you to validate their statements. They are looking for reassurance from you. If you ever feel that your validation is being sought, you can be reasonably assured that it isn't from a higher level narcissist.

People who continuously divert attention from themselves by their attempts to keep you talking about yourself are usually uncomfortable with any type of attention, especially positive. They will exhibit discomfort with compliments or an increased interest by another person. These are indications of a low self-esteem or low self-worth. This is not to say that these individuals are insincere or manipulative, they are merely attempting to keep the conversation at a comfortable level for themselves. They don't often understand how to appropriately respond to compliments or genuine interest by another person therefore they can grow quite good at steering the conversation toward the other participant.

Using the words people use to read them can become somewhat difficult at times, but as in the other methods of analyzation they can become quite useful when practiced. You need to "read between the lines" so to speak. When people use boastful language it can mean that they either need affirmation or they need you to understand how powerful they are. When people steer the conversation from themselves to you it can mean that they have a low self-esteem or it could mean that they are not ready for you to know them for the type of person they truly are. They may be trying to gain your confidence as an ally in another situation.

It's important to listen carefully to tone and inference when using words to read others. Firm tones are usually associated with demands while softer tones are associated with a desire for trust. There is your answer right there in that one sentence. Do a person's words denote a demand or a desire? Demands are absolute and unforgiving. Desires are easier to respond to as their delivery is less toxic by nature. When words instantly provoke a particular feeling within you, you need to look at both the word and the tone. This will allow you to easily identify the motive of the speaker.

Which of these sentences are you less likely to feel comfortable with?

- I need you to understand how I got the ball on my side of the court!
- The ball was on my side of the court.

Now these two sentences:

- My daughter is an excellent gymnast!
- My daughter enjoys gymnastics.

The first sentence is a demand or proclamation leaving little room for your point of view, whatever it might be. The second sentences are merely informational and tend to invite participation in the conversation. If your goal is to win the acceptance of the self-absorbed it will require that you give them what they crave or demand, and that is constant attention to them and their own importance. On the other hand, if your goal is to shut down the sociopathy associated with this type of individual, it can be a little bit more difficult. You will mainly need to strengthen your end of the conversation. Offering insights as to how others might compare to them in a positive light is less tolerable to them as well. Those who are self-absorbed will usually find another party who is willing to allow their boasting and feel more comfortable interacting with these individuals. They will rarely waste their time with someone who can offer a conversation that demands equal time and consideration.

How we respond to others is based on their words and tone. If you listen carefully to a person you can instantly understand their motives and desires all in how they present the words they speak. But don't forget that while you're learning to use words to read a person, someone else is most likely doing the same to you; quite often without even realizing it.

Chapter 6: Reading Body Language Cues and Changing your State of Mind

One major reason why people are interested in learning how to read body language and analyze people is to learn how to detect when someone is lying. This is a very understandable motivation for learning about this subject. However, it isn't as simple as being able to look at a tiny expression on someone's face or the way they move their hands and know immediately that they are lying about something. It's a bit more complicated than that, but definitely worth thinking about!

The best way to gauge a person's emotions or thoughts in the most accurate way possible is to look at how comfortable or uncomfortable they are in the moment. This spectrum of comfort and discomfort is much more reliable and important than just trying to read one expression and assume that it means something specific for every person you come across. Experts claim that people who lie (and therefore, likely feel guilty) have to walk around knowing that they are not being honest, and that this can make it hard to feel comfortable. In fact, oftentimes they are walking around with distress and tension that is visible to those who know how to spot it.

Trying to hide the fact that you're being deceptive puts a lot of stress on the brain as you struggle to come up with answers for questions that would have been easy to answer truthfully. When people are really comfortable talking to us, it's easy to tell when they are displaying signs of discomfort, which can indicate that they are not being truthful.

This means that your goal should be to get the person as comfortable as you can through building a rapport. Then you will be able to figure out how that person normally acts, or what their "baseline" of behavior and mood is. When you can familiarize yourself with the way a person appears and behaves when they aren't threatened or nervous, you can more accurately recognize when they are.

Although looking at things such as context and the situation is helpful and relevant in detecting lies, it can be used to approach every aspect of reading body language. For example, if you visit a social gathering and everyone there is chatting and having a great time, but there is one person in the corner with their head down, that person is going to stand out to you. They will probably come across as uncomfortable which will lead you to think that there is something going on with them. You may ask that person if there is something wrong with them. However, observing this exact same demeanor in a person at a hospital, for example, wouldn't raise any flags because people are often uncomfortable at hospitals.

Paying attention to someone's comfort level in a specific context offers you clues for the way they are feeling at that moment. When you're on a date with someone new and the person appears to be comfortable, you can probably assume that they like to be with you. If you are giving someone an interview for a job and the applicant looks confident and comfortable until you ask a question about their history with stealing, this is something to take note of. Although body language isn't a concrete or precise science, using some acquired knowledge in combination with your own common sense and observations about context and environment, can lead you to be pretty good at it. Then you can accurately assess what the people with you are thinking.

Most parts of our body are sending signals about what we desire or the way we feel, on a subconscious level that we often are not aware of. There are specific cues that can signal certain thoughts or ideas, but you must also keep in mind the spectrum of comfort or discomfort and remember that an isolated signal you pick up is far from the entire picture. Now let's look into some specific body parts and what signals they may be sending.

A lot of people assume that facial expressions are the most reliable or obvious indication of someone's thoughts or moods. But you should first realize, when thinking about reading someone's face, is that their facial expressions are not the most reliable gauge of their thoughts or feelings. There are a few body parts that are more honest than this, which you'll find out about soon, but let's focus on this one first. Most of us are taught starting at childhood that certain actions and facial expressions are meant for specific events or occasions, even if they are not genuine or what we really feel. This means that people give fake expressions all the time. But there are a few cues that you can still read from the face or head.

One simple body language cue to teach yourself about which isn't always easy to recognize, is a person's fake smile. A fake smile, such as one we give in social events because we "want" to be polite or because we "have" to be polite, is only visible on the mouth. Everyone knows how to do a fake smile, but not many of us realize that fake smiles do not reach our eyes. When we smile for real, our eyelids, eyebrows, and sometimes even the entire head is involved and moves upward.

Another method for recognizing when someone is growing uncomfortable is looking for pursed or tight lips on them. This can be seen in old videos of politicians admitting to something shameful, where their lips almost disappear as they give their confessions. This shows that they don't like to be saying what they are saying, and oftentimes, pursed lips show that someone is telling you only part of the truth.

These are only two simple techniques for recognizing what some facial expressions may mean, and they can reveal quite a bit about someone's true or false feelings. However, so many different variations exist that it can be more complicated than this, and as already mentioned, faces are not always reliable when it comes to body language. That's why you must pay just as much attention to the whole body, if not even more. What other body parts can you look at to tell how someone is thinking or feeling?

Although this isn't a body part that people often think about when it comes to reading people and analyzing body language, our arms are a huge part of expressing feelings and thoughts. A lot of gestures and expressions are trained or taught to us throughout life, like the fact that it's rude to point. Apart from these obvious social norms, there are some other considerations to make about arms when trying to read someone's moods. Look at how much room or space they are taking up with their arms, and also how high their arms are reaching.

Gestures that seem to defy gravity, no matter what body part it happens in, are typically positive. As soon as someone becomes interested, excited, or happy, their arms rise, their chins and heads go up, and even their feet or legs might start to bounce or point upward. A person's arms are especially versatile when it comes to reading this behavior. When we're happy or excited our arm movements are unrestricted and we may raise them over our heads. A happy and energized person makes motions that go against gravity with their arms. This is easy to remember since someone feeling "up" means they are happy, while the opposite means that they feel the opposite. When someone is in a confident mood, they affirmatively swing their arms as they walk, while an insecure person will keep their arms restrained as if gravity is pulling them downward.

If you tell a co-worker about a costly and drastic mistake they made while working, their arms and shoulders will visibly droop and sink. Negative emotions cause all of our body parts to experience gravity more, which is why we call them "sinking" feelings. These responses are automatic, subconscious, and happen immediately. For instance, right when our team scores a goal, we punch our hands into the air. These behaviors accurately show our feelings at the exact moment that we feel them. In addition to this, these signals might affect those around us and become contagious. Smaller hand gestures can help show specific, conscious concepts, such as the "thumbs up" sign, or a wave, but if you want to look deeper and get to the comfort level or subconscious moods of someone, pay attention to the gravity of their arms and body in general.

The middle of our body or torso (made up of the belly, chest, and shoulders) is absolutely vital for our wellness and general survival. This is where most of our important organs are, and so we have a subconscious need to protect this area at all times, instinctively. But this isn't only apparent in body language when we are in physically threatening or safe situations. This applies even in more relaxed social environments. To put it plainly, we leave our torsos free and open when we feel comfortable with the situation or person.

Our torsos show our limbic brain's desire to avoid and distance ourselves when we are feeling threatened. For example, if someone feels as though there is something wrong in their relationship, they are probably picking up on this degree of distance from their loved one and reacting to it, even if they aren't consciously aware that this is what is actually happening. This distancing might also mean that they are showing ventral (or front) denial. The fronts of our bodies are sensitive to our likes and dislikes. When something is going well, we will turn these parts to what we like, including situations or people. If something is going wrong, on the other hand, we turn away or shift in the opposite direction.

The front side of our bodies is by far the most vulnerable, so our subconscious and limbic brain feels a need to automatically protect it from threat. This is why we start to turn our sides a bit when we get approached by someone we don't want to talk to at a social gathering, for example. When you are observing people in situations involving dating or courtship, this is a highly reliable indicator of whether the relationship is going well or not. Either denying or sharing the front of your body with others is most obviously observed when it comes to romantic or dating situations. When a couple is new, they usually angle their torsos toward each other, rather than away from each other. This happens when they're sitting down, standing, or one of them walks into a room.

This happens because they are comfortable with each other, have a favorable standing, and so their bodies don't have to protect their limbic systems. When we deny or protect access to the center of our bodies is when we encounter unpleasant or threatening situations or people. When we leave our abdomen and chest open, or point them to someone, we feel safe and happy with the situation.

You might be surprised to find out that you can actually tell a lot about someone's internal state by what their legs are doing. But this is actually where the most honesty can be found. While some may believe that the face is a good indicator, this is the part of our bodies that we have been trained and conditioned to lie about our emotions with. We grew up being told to smile, look friendly, or quit making silly faces. But countless years of human evolution have ingrained within us that our legs must be ready, at a moment's notice, to escape danger.

The simplest, and most reliable, method for figuring out someone's feelings or intentions by looking at their legs to see which direction the feet are pointing in. Just like the way we angle our torsos away from or toward people, our lower bodies usually point or lean toward the way we want to go, or the direction we're interested in. When people are having a conversation, they are usually talking with their toes pointed toward each other. But if one of them starts to turn their feet away or points one foot outward, this is a sign that they want to walk away or go somewhere else. This behavior of the feet is a sign or a signal of intention. Someone's torso might point in the direction of someone they don't like out of feeling consciously obligated, but a person's feet are honestly reflecting the brain's desire to stay or escape the situation or person.

On the other hand, if someone has their legs crossed, especially as they are standing up, this is a strong signal that they want to stay put. Again, this comes from our basic subconscious need to survive and protect our best interests. Even if we are pretending that we're having fun in a situation, crossed feet or legs means that it would take us a lot longer to escape from a threatening or dangerous situation. Even if someone is consciously aware that they aren't in actual physical danger, our brains will still react as if there's a physical threat when we want to leave a social situation.

One aspect of reading body language cues that you can't escape or ignore is first establishing a person's baseline. This is the most crucial aspect of analyzing people. All individuals have their personal habits and quirks. Someone who is shy, for example, might normally hold their arms close to themselves and keep their heads down, even in normal situations. A "leader", on the other hand, will do the opposite. While people who don't know them well may take these signals to assume that they are going through a unique emotional state, it's actually just showing their default body language. A single isolated behavior doesn't necessarily show that there has been a change in someone's mood.

As you become more familiar with someone, however, and the way they act in typical situations, unusual behavior can serve as a far more reliable indication of the way they feel at that moment. Don't only keep an eye out for someone with their head up or their legs crossed, as this may be default behavior that just signals what their personality or usual demeanor is like. Instead, pay attention to something they do that is outside of the way they usually behave.

Many times, you don't have to look very deep to find out what someone is reacting to or figure out what they're thinking. If they seem calm and happy one moment, and then make a pained face when a certain person walks up, you can safely assume that the person caused this reaction. You should rely on your own instincts, context, and feelings, in addition to these body language signals, which can mean many different things. The only way to get a full picture is to use a combination of methods.

Body language is important not only for deciphering what the people around you are feeling and thinking, but for changing your own state of mind or sending the right signals to the people around you. Part of becoming a master of analyzing others is learning how to improve the body language cues you are using on a daily basis. Using body language effectively can determine whether your interactions with people go well or fall flat. Here are some useful tips and tricks for sending strong signals in nonverbal communication.

Research has proven that when you hold yourself in a "powerful" or expansive pose (such as standing with your arms open or leaning on a desk with your feet apart) for a couple of minutes, your body will begin to create more testosterone. This means that you instantly start to feel more in control, dominant, and powerful. When you are feeling doubtful or nervous about your confidence but want to either seem self-assured or make yourself feel better, assume poses like this. People will respond more to their personal feelings about you than the words you choose to use, another reason why body language matters a lot.

In order to encourage others to participate and speak up more, make sure that you are not multitasking when they talk, which can be seen as very discouraging, to some. Although it can be tempting to look at the clock or check your email, you need to show that you're listening to get people to open up. You can do this by making sure you are facing them with your whole body and looking them in the eye. Tilting your face, nodding, and leaning forward are also good signals to send that show you're listening and paying close attention to what they're saying. While listening and hearing are important, showing that you are doing these things is equally important.

Obstructions can be a huge detriment to collaborating with people. If you are talking to someone and you want them to collaborate or work together with you on something, remove anything that may be forming a barrier or blocking your view of them. Even on breaks at work or in meetings, be aware that holding something in front of you can be subconsciously interpreted as you trying to distance yourself from someone or block your view of them. People who feel comfortable in social environments hold their hands at a lower level, than those who feel insecure or threatened.

Physical touch is a powerful and primitive body language cue to use. If you touch someone on the shoulder, hand or arm, it can create a warmer bond, but only if they are comfortable with it. Of course, you should use your best judgment for when this would be well received or not. In a professional environment, warmth and touch are typically established using handshaking, and even this small amount of contact can create a positive, lasting impression on the other person. When you shake someone's hand, you are twice as likely to remember them, and see them as friendly and open people.

A real genuine smile can not only heighten your feelings of happiness, but it can send the right messages to the people around you. A smile indicates that you are trustworthy, cooperative, and approachable. A true smile will light up your face, crinkle your eyes, come on slow and leave slowly. Smiling influences the way those near you will respond to you. When we give someone else a smile, they almost always give one back, and since body language or expressions affect mental states, this can leave them with a positive impression or mood.

When businesspeople or clients imitate your nonverbal cues subconsciously, they are sending signals that they either agree with you or like you on a personal level. When you consciously and purposely "mirror" those around you, it can cause them to feel a strong rapport with you. Paying attention to someone's body language and expressions, mirroring them subtly and naturally will help them feel accepted and understood by you. Be careful, however, not to go overboard on this, as this will cause the opposite effect you're hoping for.

Gesturing is linked with speaking, and using more gestures as we talk can add fuel to our thinking and articulation. Try this out and you will notice that when you use your hands as you talk, you have a clearer mind and can find the words you're searching for more easily. Many people do this without even being aware of it, but consciously using it to your advantage will get you far.

If you hope to come across as authoritative or respectable to those you speak with, you should be conscious of the pitch of your voice. When we're nervous, we might talk too loud, too quietly, too high or too low. This is a habit you should work on for maximizing good impressions. Before you are making a phone call or going into an interview, practice keeping your voice at an even pitch. Don't talk too loud, too fast, or too unevenly, and you will send the message that you are confident and capable of whatever you're about to do.

If you are hoping to be more effective at storing important memories, try uncrossing your legs and arms as you listen. This can also be used to help people interact more in a meeting or conference. If you notice a lot of people are sitting with crossed legs or arms, encourage them to stand up, move around, and interact with the environment. This will automatically cause them to feel more engaged and involved, and all around more positive about the experience.

Now that you have a better understanding of body language and how it affects communication, as well as its ability to change your frame of mind, you'll need to use it in practice yourself and try to identify it in others as they interact. While there are many different facets involved with body language and interpreting its meaning it is a knowledge base that can be easy to learn if you continue to practice.

Don't get so caught up in the terminology that you forget how much of this is already planted in your subconscious. Many of us have this so ingrained that we take it for granted and forget that it is actually imbedded in our minds. We commonly watch people interact during most phases of our day, and if you think about it you are usually assessing or analyzing these people without even thinking about it. It's usually when force the issue that we over complicate the ability to do this naturally.

Conclusion

Thanks again for purchasing this book. I hope that you were able to gain valuable insights as to how to recognize certain personality types and what this can help you realize about individuals. In addition to this, hopefully you understood the benefits that can become apparent to you by mastering the art of reading body language. You can now start enjoying these benefits:

- **Controlling your Body Language for the Best Results:** Most of us know the way we want to come across and seem to others, but not how to do it. Now that you've read this book, you're equipped with the knowledge you need to effectively send the signals you want to send. Whether it's a job interview you want to master, showing your boss that you're capable of taking on more responsibility, or getting someone to accept a date with you, now you can do it.

- **Understanding Others:** One of life's most confusing and mysterious subjects is trying to read other people. Now that you have the information given to you in this guide, you can look deeper than someone's smile or frown and get to know what they are really feeling deep inside. You can use this information to deepen relationships, make new friends, or score more professional opportunities in the workplace.

- **Impressing People with your Knowledge:** Many people aren't good at listening, paying attention to others, or reading them accurately. If you are one of the few who can master this subject, you will impress people by how much you notice and see. Since impressions go a long way in all areas of life, this is a valuable skill to have.

As with any other skill, reading nonverbal cues and body language is something that you need to test out as often as possible in order to get better with it. The more you practice at this, the easier it will get.

Book #2

How to Analyze People

How to Master Reading Anyone Instantly Using Body Language, Human Psychology, and Personality Types

Introduction: The Importance of Analyzing Others Instantly

When communicating with others, we have become extraordinarily dependent upon just what we see and hear on the surface. However, just below the shallows is a whole other world of motivations that direct behaviors and determine the effectiveness of our perceptions. Often others' surface expressions, words, and actions are not congruent to what is happening on that deeper level. To be dynamic communicators, we need to have "deep see" vision to analyze others real motives and reason behind what they say and do. Not only will analyzing others give us a more accurate perception of them, but it will also give us greater insight into ourselves.

Have you ever felt an almost uncanny creepiness about a person or an immediate kinship with someone, but you have no clear explanation as to why? That's because you were sensitive to other non-verbal signals, behaviors, and traits that the other person was so desperately wanting to hide to gain your trust. Once you train yourself to be mindful of others' covert messages, you'll have much more confidence in your perceptions and ability to handle almost any situation before it becomes threatening to your well-being. So, let's look at what learning to analyze others can do for us.

Accurately Analyzing Others Can Keep Us Physically Safe

Linda is an excellent example of how carefully analyzing others can protect you. As a Realtor® for over ten years, Linda attributed much of her success on her strong communication skills. She had been told on numerous occasions that she was a good judge of character, and it had paid off in spades. When she was with clients, it was as if she knew what her prospects were going to say or do before they knew. One afternoon, these skills served a far greater purpose than merely winning her the contract.

Each morning she had coffee on her way to work. It was a great way to socialize and pass out her business cards. As Linda waited in line for her coffee, she struck up a conversation with the gentleman behind her. As usual, she gave him her business card, and he immediately shared his need to sell his home and move into something larger. He had just been promoted at work and wanted his lifestyle to reflect his new position, and Linda was eager to help him search for the perfect home. He gave her his address, and they arranged to meet the next day at his home with a current market analysis to determine its value.

Never suspecting danger, Linda went by herself to his home, knocked at the front door with her usual confidence, and waited for his invitation to enter. He welcomed her into the home and stepped behind her to lock the front door. She immediately felt this was a bit odd but dispelled the feeling in hopes that it was out of habit rather than a need to trap her inside his home. As she looked around, she noticed no sign of a feminine touch, with the minimal furnishings showing nothing but masculine appeal.

Unable to rid herself of the creep factor, Linda began to ask questions. "I'm ashamed of myself, but I didn't even get your name yesterday." She held out her hand to introduce herself—"Hi, I'm Linda, and, you are?"

"Oh—Jeff. My name's, Umm, Jeff," he replied, as he looked down at his feet. As if remembering he should behave differently, Jeff then looked up and smiled and offered his hand. That's when Linda noticed something else that was odd. His hand was clammy as if his nerves were getting the better of him. Upon closer inspection, she also noticed that although Jeff offered a smile in response, it was tight and didn't reach all the way to his eyes.

"Hello, Jeff," she smiled back, trying not to show her nervousness. "Do you mind if I look around so I can get an idea of the value of your house?"

"Oh, right—right," he said, walking behind her in a herding manner, and moving closely behind her toward the hallway.

"Well, let's start out here in the living area and kitchen, shall we?" As she passed the hall, her neck hairs began to stand to attention, and she went on full alert. The first room to the right of the hallway was entirely black, and she caught a glimpse of the corner of a daybed with a pink boa draped across its sidearm. It was difficult for Linda to hide her dismay at the sight of this little island of femininity in Jeff's otherwise overly masculine house.

Linda continued to take notes as she walked around the kitchen, asking light questions to try to keep the conversation casual. The quieter the two of them became, the louder Linda's little voice in her head shouted for her to get out of there. "You know, it got chilly this morning. I have such allergies in changing weather like this. Would you have some tissue?"

"Oh, yeah, he moved once again to position himself at her back awkwardly. Come on back," he said, as he then moved around her to walk down the hallway.

"Why don't you get some, and I'll get my jacket in the car?" The moment Jeff began walking down the hall, Linda made her getaway. Thankfully, she maneuvered herself between Jeff and the locked front door but opened the deadbolt quickly. She quickly grabbed her briefcase and car keys from the side table, ran to her car, and pulled out of Jeff's driveway as if the devil himself were after her.

Upset and shaken, Linda immediately reported her fear and behavior to her broker, warning other females not to go to that address alone. She wanted to call the police, but there was nothing to report, so she shook off her feeling of foreboding and took off the rest of the afternoon. Three nights later, Linda realized how close she had come to the horrific realization of her feelings that all was not as it should be at Jeff's house. As she watched the 10:00 news, she saw police leading Jeff out of his house in handcuffs, and the anchor people sadly reported his connection to two murdered women on the west side of the city.

Linda called the police and shared her story, and as she told them what happened, she realized that her analysis of Jeff had been spot on, but it was not what he said that had tipped her off to his possible deviant plans. It was how he behaved, what she observed, and her overall perceptions that signaled the alarm. Linda knew that she had always been able to read others well, but this time her intuitive perceptions had done more than fund her life—they had saved her life!

Analyzing Others Can Bring Us Professional Prosperity

James had never considered himself a natural born leader, but he had been asked to act as company vice president after the unexpected departure of his boss. He dreaded the first office meeting when he would have to share with the team that he was now the new vice president. James just knew that everybody had loved Eddie. He had a quick wit and a welcoming smile, always inviting others to participate and share their feelings about any new ideas or required changes. He gave the salespeople full reign to do their thing, and the team seemed to enjoy the freedom.

James, on the other hand, was a quiet contemplator. He knew that his discomfort with public speaking and quick decision making had negatively impacted several potential promotions for him throughout the years. Now that James finally had the opportunity to lead, he couldn't help but feel out of his comfort zone. James was shocked that he had been chosen for the position, and second to his disbelief was his feelings of inadequacy and unpreparedness. Just two months previously, James had attended a communications seminar where the speaker talked about the effects of misunderstandings in the workplace. Now James wondered if others would mistake his quiet demeanor and reticent manner as a lack of leadership skills.

James welcomed the opportunity to promote his assistant to become the new executive assistant to the vice president, knowing her strengths were his weaknesses. She was confident, outgoing, and easily trusted when James tended to hang back. Yes, Susan would be the perfect complement to him in this new position, and he looked forward to having her input. As it turned out, James fears were put to rest when the team began to flourish under his gentle guidance and Susan's nurturing nature.

Together, they created stability in the sales team and encouraged even greater participation and higher-level contributions from all parties. It seemed the wrong perceptions were on James part. What he believed everybody thought was real leadership had been a gathering of the "good ole boys" club, where little was expected and even less achieved. In record time, the salespeople thrived under James leadership and his assistant's support. James' confidence and performance were surprisingly successful in creating peak performance for the entire team, and he and Susan worked together to build the highest selling team in the company.

There are many other ways analyzing people can benefit you. Learn and apply the strategies in our book, and you'll gain a new perspective on yourself and others. When you begin reading others and yourself with an open mind and willing spirit, your new skills will lead you to even greater successes in your personal and professional lives. Your relationships will improve, your confidence will increase, and your analytical knowledge will open doors for you that you never dreamed possible.

Analyzing Others Can Give Insight in Your Personal Relationships

For the longest time, the HOA board meetings had consisted of Ally and her husband. Until Theresa came along, nobody had been interested in the need to keep the greenbelts clean and the streetlights were working. Ally was a contradiction of feelings; although it was great to have another's opinion, she felt somewhat uncomfortable around Theresa. After the board meeting one evening, Theresa was on her way home when Ally's husband offered her a ride.

Nothing seemed out of the ordinary on the surface, but Ally felt wary of Theresa around her husband, Eddie. When she voiced her feelings to Eddie, he brushed her off and said something sarcastic about seeing her claws come out whenever Theresa was in the room. The more Ally tried not to let things bother her, the more the thoughts rolled around in her head. Perhaps it was because Eddie had worked so much overtime the last two weeks, and his boss was so selfish in his overtime pay that created such suspicious thoughts in Ally.

The next morning, Ally was checking the sprinklers out front when her neighbor walked over and told her something that confirmed her fears. The friend told Ally she had asked Eddie to say hello the other night when he was standing outside Theresa's house. "Oh, what night was that?" Ally asked.

"I went by the night before last, and he was standing outside Theresa's with a big box in his hands. I wondered if she was moving."

"I don't know." Ally was so upset that she excused herself and went into the house quickly before her neighbor could see her tears. The rest of the day was spent wondering what she was going to do. She wasn't going to put up with a cheating husband, but she just couldn't imagine herself without Eddie. It was her birthday, no less, and Eddie hadn't even wished her a happy birthday before going to work that morning. She just could face the heartache of telling him she knew, so she left before he could get home. As Ally passed Theresa's street, she noticed Eddie's car parked in front. Too hurt to stop and too mad not to, Ally decided she would put an end to this behavior and stop Eddie in his tracks.

She quickly ran to the front door, not realizing what a mess she looked with her makeup smeared and her hair still wet at the temples for trying to clean her face up before leaving the house. Nobody answered, so she rang the doorbell once again, and this time Eddie came to the door. "What are you doing here, honey?" Eddie took one look at her and knew she must be having an emergency. "What's wrong? Are you hurt?"

"You might say that, Eddie." Ally waved her arms in the air and continued with "I'm hurt about all this. How could you do this?" she asked, before bursting into tears.

Eddie grabbed her by the arm and pulled her into Theresa's house. "Okay, okay, what's all this about? What do you think I'm doing?"

"I've seen how you two look at each other as if you've got a secret you don't want anybody else to know about."

Theresa came out from the other room and walked over to Ally, "We do. We've been planning your surprise birthday party for the past two weeks."

Ally's misunderstanding had caused her pain and hurt, and it could have been the end of her marriage. Relationships are made and broken by poor communications and false perceptions. We would probably be shocked at how many couples had split because of mistaken beliefs caused by unfounded suspicions, as well as how many others were able to mislead their significant other and hold a shaky relationship together through deceit and negative manipulation.

These are the reasons we've written this book on how to analyze others. You'll learn to be more decisive, and rely on your perceptions to give you clarity in your personal and professional life. It won't take long before the benefits of that "deeper see" vision pays off in longer-lasting, more rewarding relationships and more profitable business associations. So, let's get started, shall we?

Chapter 1: Identifying Personality Types

Even though there are four main personality types, most people are a combination of two or more types. You might be primarily one type with a few traits of another, or you could be middle of the road between two different types. There are also some people who have a few traits of every type. Several things determine your personality types, but the strongest influences are typically one's upbringing, hormones, and chemical makeup.

If you read my other book *How to Analyze People: How to Read Anyone Instantly Using Body Language, Personality Types and Human Psychology,* then you might already be familiar with these four personality types. In this chapter, we'll review the different personality types and go into greater detail about the positive and negative traits of each types, and their identifying behaviors and language.

Knowing others personality types and identifying behaviors and language that are characteristic of these types of people will help you know how best to relate to them in your personal and professional endeavors. After you have studied the personality types, take the time to do a personal inventory to discover your personality type. Knowing how you prefer to relate to others and how they want you to relate to them is paramount in making the necessary adjustments to the way you communicate with people of all different personality types and traits.

The Leader Personality Type

Leader Personality Types make great presidents and executives, administrators and wall street moguls, or managers and supervisors. Many politicians are Leader Personalities as well.

Positive Traits of a Leader Personality Type

Confident	Direct	Strategic	Problem-Solver
Decisive	Driven	Courageous	Bold
Independent	Goal-Oriented	Money-Oriented	Proud
Energetic	Focused	Competitive	Hard-Working
Powerful	Tough	Determined	Take Charge

Negative Traits of a Leader Personality Type

Tense	Workaholic	Opinionated	Temperamental
Stressed	Too Controlling	Power Hungry	Too Authoritative
Unforgiving	Rude	Aggressive	Judging
Distrusting	Unavailable	Detached	Unsocial
Impatient	Self-Centered	Overly Competitive	Stubborn

Identifying Behaviors of a Leader Personality Type

- They don't take a lot of time for family and friends.
- Most of their conversations center around work and money-making ventures.
- They respect strength and competitiveness, so they will usually be sports-minded and fit.
- They have a strong, confident handshake.
- Since they are money-motivated, they will usually drive an expensive car, live in a luxurious estate, and wear designer watches.
- They don't have much patience with people who don't display appreciation for the finer things in life.
- They are attracted to intelligent people and usually will not associate with others whom they feel are not on their level.
- Their body language is often a wide stance with arms folded in front of them or braced at the waist.
- It will be difficult for them to focus on conversations that don't center around work or intellectual matters.

Identifying Language of a Leader Personality Type

I   My   Intellect   Ambition   Challenge

The Identifier Personality Type

Identifier Personality Types are especially caring and nurturing people. They love nothing more than to educate, help, or heal others. These personality types make outstanding teachers, nurses, and counselors.

Positive Traits of an Identifier Personality Type

Nurturing	Encouraging	Sympathetic	Cooperative
Understanding	Relational	Expressive	Unassuming
Considerate	Charitable	Soul Searching	Trusting
Good Listeners	Compassionate	Agreeable	Empathetic
Emotional	Imaginative	Idealistic	Contributors

Negative Traits of an Identifier Personality Type

Over-Thinkers	Drama Queens	Sacrificial	Imbalanced Lifestyle
Appear Needy	Too Agreeable	Indecisive	Demand Reassurance
Unfocused	Too Accepting	Take on Problems of the Universe	

Identifying Behaviors of an Identifier Personality Type

- Because Identifier Personality Types don't want to offend others, they are often too agreeable.
- They are most susceptible to suffering depression or moodiness.

- They do not take criticism well; they become too easily offended.
- If they are in a managing position, they prefer an open-door policy.
- Their managing style is more open and relaxed.
- If they fear confrontation or rejection in social situations, they can appear shy and timid.
- Their body language is usually open arms and trusting mannerisms.
- They can be a bit touch-feely for other's taste.
- They are comfortable talking about emotions and their warm and fuzzy conversations often center around feelings and charitable events.

Identifying Language of an Identifier Personality Type

| Passion | Sensitive | Sweet | Understand | Sorry |

The Fraternizer Personality Type

Fraternizer Personality Types enjoy high adventure and challenging themselves with almost everything. They are real sensation seekers whose hunger for the unconventional adventure is their ultimate enjoyment. You will usually find Fraternizer Personality Types working as comedians, entertainers, event planners, venue coordinators, or even travel guides.

Positive Traits of a Fraternizer Personality Type

Friendly	Storytellers	Energetic	Charming
Spontaneous	Curious	Engaging	Outspoken
Social Butterfly	Outgoing	Optimistic	Adaptable
Conversationalist	Athletic	Humorous	Fun-loving
Enthusiastic	Knowledgeable	Creative	Unconventional

Negative Traits of a Fraternizer Personality Type

Too Talkative	Doesn't Listen	Self-Centered	Unfocused
Easily Bored	Impulsive	Restless	Self-Absorbed
Procrastinator	Low Tolerance	Scattered	Uncalculated Risk Taker

Identifying Behaviors of a Fraternizer Personality Type

- They love to travel and talk about their adventures.
- Fraternizers enjoy outdoor adventures, and they're always up for something out-of-the-norm.
- They are not afraid to speak their minds, even if they hold the unpopular opinion. Usually, they get others to agree with them just because they are so likable.
- They are big spenders. Fraternizers will usually pick up the tab for dinner or drinks.
- Because they are so impulsive and social, they are often more susceptible to drug and alcohol abuse.
- It can be challenging getting them to settle down to find a solution to a pressing problem.
- Most Fraternizers have bigger-than-life gestures and expressions.

Identifying Language of a Fraternizer Personality Type

Adventure	Energy	New	Fun	Wealthy
Pleasure	Happiness	Travel	Active	Why Not?

The Perceiver Personality Type

Perceiver Personality Types are your more serious-minded of the four main personality types. Because they are so fact-driven, they are quite often engineers, mathematicians, scientists, and technology experts.

Positive Traits of a Perceiver Personality Type

Organized	Purpose-Driven	Concentrated	Logical
Analytical	Task-Oriented	Factual	Orderly
Predictable	Detail-Oriented	Structured	Dependable
Deep Thinker	Investigative	Patient	Persistent
Sentimental	Respectful	Reliable	Planner

Negative Traits of a Perceiver Personality Type

Unemotional	Too One-minded	Loner	Too Serious
Unsocial	Cold	Predictable	Anxious
Dogmatic	Hard to Please	Obsessive	Stubborn

Identifying Behaviors of a Perceiver Personality Type

- Since they value being thoughtful and self-controlled, they express themselves using very precise language.
- They don't work well with demanding deadlines, and they are challenged with high-pressure tasks.
- They can be obsessive/compulsive in their behaviors.
- They can often be judging and critical of others.
- They are uncomfortable being the center of attention, so you will usually find them standing in the back of the group or crowd.
- They don't know how to take compliments and show embarrassment when given one.
- Since they are such deep thinkers, they don't usually make quick decisions or act quickly in an urgent situation.
- Perceivers will be the ones who hold you up in the grocery line to count out the exact change.
- Their body language is closed, and you will often notice that they avoid making eye contact.

Identifying Language of a Perceiver Personality Type

Respect   Moral   Loyalty   Careful   Count on Me

Taking a Personal Inventory of Your Personality Type

Answer the following questions to discover your personality type or types. Circle the letter that best describes your feelings, thoughts, or behaviors in the given situations. When you have completed the personal inventory, tally up your points to see your most likely personality type(s).

1. When you're in a meeting, you usually...

    a. Try to get everybody to participate

    b. Be quiet and let others do the talking

    c. Act like I agree even if I don't so I won't be confrontational

    d. Offer my feelings on the subject and encourage others to as well

2. If your significant other is angry or frustrated, you ...

    a. Suggest an evening out on the town to relieve the stress

    b. Go to my office for a while until he or she cools down

    c. Feel bad and wonder what I did wrong

    d. Let them think it out and then ask some pointed questions to seek closure

3. If your computer is acting up, you most likely would...

    a. Search the manual or the Internet for the problem, carefully weigh the suggested remedies, and then try the most likely solution

b.   Call a friend to come over for a drink and see what they can do to help me fix it

c.   I get the IT guy at work to come over and fix it

d.   I chat online and see if others are having the same issues and then try some of the things that helped them overcome the problem

4. If you get stood up for an evening out, what do you do?

   a.   Call another friend and go somewhere with them instead.

   b.   I enjoy the evening by myself at home.

   c.   I ask them if there is anything I can do to help them with whatever it was that kept them from enjoying an evening with me.

   d.   I do some work at home and get a head start on the next day's tasks.

5. When you lose a bet or a competition of some kind, you might…

   a.   Double down—I hate to lose

   b.   Wonder if they somehow cheated

   c.   Be happy for my competitor

   d.   Laugh it off and get ready for the next bet

6. If someone tries to tell you what to do, you usually …

   a.   Listen to what they say, and then figure it out for myself anyway

   b.   Understand they have experienced this before and try to do what they suggest

   c.   I think they've got their nerve and do what I want

   d.   Make a joke about it and then wait until they leave and ask someone else to do it for me

7. If you told your significant other you didn't want a dog and he or she got one anyway, you would most likely...

   a. Smile and start playing with the dog.

   b. Try to be sensitive to their need for a dog and think of how I can help take care of it

   c. Remember what happened the last time he or she got a dog and then remind them of what a disaster it was

   d. Make them take the dog back from whence it came

8. If you paid to have your car detailed and they didn't do a good job, you would most likely...

   a. Realize that they usually did a good job and just live with it

   b. Be upset with them and make them do the whole thing over

   c. Kid around with them and ask them to touch it up in spots

   d. I would give myself time to think about what I wanted to say and then take it back the next day and ask them to make it right

9. If you were dressed for and on your way to work and saw that your car had a flat tire in the driveway, you would...

   a. Call a company to fix the tire and work from home until it was repaired

   b. Call a friend or my significant other and ask what I should do

   c. Call into work and let them know, call a repair company, and then go for a run until it was fixed

   d. Look at the tire to see if it was tampered with, and then have it fixed, but I would be watching the street to see if anyone else was having a similar problem

10. If your child got a poor grade on his or her report card, AGAIN, you would most likely…

   a. Sit down with them and listen to their explanation and then figure out with them how they could do better next time

   b. Depend on my significant other to handle the situation

   c. Offer them some money to do better

   d. Probably blow up and let them know who's boss

Scoring—Discover Your Personality Type(s)

Give yourself a point under each appropriate personality type and then tally your points to see what personality type is dominant and which ones are secondary.

Question	Leader	Identifier	Fraternizer	Perceiver
#1	a	b	d	c
#2	b	c	a	d
#3	c	d	b	a
#4	d	c	a	b
#5	a	c	d	b
#6	c	b	d	a
#7	d	b	a	c
#8	b	a	c	d
#9	a	b	c	d
#10	d	a	c	b
Total				

Under which personality type(s) did you have the most circles? The personality type with the most circles is probably your dominant personality type, and those with just a few circles have some influence in your behaviors and beliefs.

Now comes the big surprise. Even though you took this Personal Inventory and you "think" you are predominantly one personality type, you might find out differently when it comes to what you'll discover in the next chapter. It's all about perception. How you perceived yourself might be much different than how others see you. So, let's explore the principles of perception and see what influence these perceptions have on the way we analyze ourselves and others.

Chapter 2: The Principles of Perceptions

As you analyze others and yourself, you begin to form temporary and long-lasting perceptions. These truths are invaluable to get an accurate read of others and examine what motivates others' behaviors and beliefs. However, there are some universal truths about perceptions, and we call these the Principles of Perceptions. As you read others' body language and analyze their behaviors, keep the following Five Principles of Perceptions in mind. Knowing them will help your analysis to be more accurate.

Principle #1: Perceptions Are Deceptive

There is much information that goes into your analysis of yourself and others. However, it's not good practice to blindly accept the information that filters through your mind to create your perceptions. Why? To form your opinions of others while you analyze their behaviors and beliefs, you are working with a limited amount of knowledge and awareness. The following strategies will offer a more accurate analysis and verify or replace your initial perceptions.

- Spending more time with the people you are analyzing to form your impressions gives you a more precise read on their behaviors and beliefs. When you jump to conclusions about what motivates people to say or do things, you are playing off old tapes of past experiences. Your judgments can be tainted because of previous experiences you had when another person said or did similar things.

- Observing how others react to the people you are reading helps you to know whether you are too critical or judging of them. You need to ask yourself if your opinions of this person are based on personal likes or dislikes, or are your perceptions based on unbiased observations and effective listening skills.

- Have you rushed to judgment? When you are analyzing others, give them time to prove or disprove your perceptions of them. Avoid forming your analysis on just one or two encounters. If you must analyze another's behavior quickly, realize that there's a good chance your perceptions will not be entirely accurate.

Principle #2: Background Brings Accuracy

There are times when you must analyze others' behaviors quickly, but when you do your perceptions might be off the mark. After all, you have no background on this person and no history with which to form your impressions. For example, if you are in a group and someone moves away from you to stand on the other side of the group, what do you think? If you rush to judgment, you might believe that they are giving you the cold shoulder. Or, if you have experienced recent rejection, you might begin to wonder what is wrong with you. What you don't know when analyzing others can and will hurt your ability to form accurate perceptions.

Let's say this situation goes a little further and the person you are examining turns her head away from you. It's easy to convince yourself she is avoiding you—until you find out later in the evening that your subject suffered a severe hearing loss and needed to move closer to the speaker and tilt her head to hear better from her functioning ear. Suddenly, your perceptions of that person have drastically changed. Why? You have more background information.

Principle #3: Awareness & Accuracy Go Hand-in-Hand

The reason you need to be familiar with the four personality types, observe others' body language, and listen to the words they frequently use is because awareness gives you a broader and more accurate picture of what motivates them to act and say what they do. There is greater awareness when you gain more knowledge and apply that knowledge to what you see and hear. While you can observe behaviors, if you don't know the cause of the behavior, it's just empty information.

You can be aware of how others stand, sit, walk, and communicate, but if you don't know what these signals mean, the information is no use to you. Your perceptions of people continue to form based on nothing more than your past experiences, which give you a limited, one-dimensional picture. When you can combine your past experiences and motivations to a greater knowledge of what's behind these behaviors and words, then your relationships will magically improve, and your actions and beliefs will change as well.

If you want to increase your awareness and apply it to your analysis of others, you've come to the right place. Educating yourself on reading body language and recognizing personality types will enable you to achieve more efficient communications with people much different from yourself. Most people tend to form relationships with individuals who are like them, so learning to monitor and adjust your behaviors and words to match another will draw others to you.

Principle #4: Position Alters Perception

All of us would like to believe that our perceptions and analysis are not unduly influenced by another's position, but the truth of the matter is that we are all impressed or turned off by others based on many different criteria. Much of what impacts our analysis has nothing to do with how they behave or what they say. Many perceptions are the results of the other person's position in life. Being influenced by another's position in life doesn't mean that every person who has a big title is automatically respected because some people resent others' success. The following are some things that alter perceptions.

- Career Choice
- Company
- Job Title
- Your Bosses' Favored-Peer
- Other Friends or Acquaintances Who Page Homage to Their Authority

If your perception of another is that they are above or below your status, then your analysis of that person will be impacted by your perception. If you review the personality types, you'll notice that Leader and Perceiver Personalities can be more judging than Fraternizers and Identifiers. Knowing you are a Leader Personality Type can help you to understand that you often allow others' positions to get in the way of your analysis and influence your beliefs about them. Gaining this knowledge about your personality type makes you more aware of how you respond to others' behaviors and beliefs, thereby creating better relationships.

Principle #5: We See What We Want to See

Have you ever noticed how what you expect to happen almost always happens? Well, this is no coincidence. Expectations influence our analysis of others' behaviors and words. In other words, we see what we want to see, especially if our emotions are involved. If we are in a highly emotional state, it's difficult to see past the anger, love, or fear.

Analysis based on emotion is not just slightly inaccurate, but those perceptions are often so slanted that when you share your thoughts with others, they think you've lost touch with reality. I'm sure you have heard of all the romance scams happening online these days. Men and women are being swindled out of hundreds of thousands of dollars because they are in a vulnerable state and allow another person to take advantage of them. There are now scammers who have developed "so-called" services that say they can help reveal a possible scammer. That's the web emotions can weave when it comes to analyzing the behaviors and motives of those we think we know.

Some people with a terminal illness believe they can be cured by a concoction provided through someone who claims to be a doctor. Unfortunately, this is what happened to Carl. Carl's specialist diagnosed him with third-stage cancer. His prognosis wasn't promising, but when Carl could not accept the hopelessness of his situation, he contacted a doctor he heard of who had experienced incredible results with his treatment of cancer. Carl spent thousands of dollars traveling to India, and thousands more staying at the doctor's treatment center. The treatments were uncomfortable, and they kept Carl away from his family for weeks at a time, but at the end of each treatment, Carl felt better for a while.

The doctor told Carl that it would take several treatments before he would experience lasting results, and each time Carl would see what he wanted to see. Although his family saw him getting weaker, thinner, and less energetic, Carl saw himself as more fit and in a calmer state of mind. Just days after his last treatment, Carl died of cancer, and his family felt cheated out of the time they could have spent with him during his final year of life. How could an otherwise intelligent, professional man have been so fooled? It's easy; he allowed his highly emotional state to override his better judgment. He wanted the treatments to work so badly, that he was victim to the fifth principle of perceptions—we see what we want to see.

The Importance of Knowing the Five Principles of Perception

To read and analyze others accurately, you must first understand how perceptions influence behaviors and beliefs and then judge the accuracy of your feelings. It just doesn't help to read one's body language if you don't realize your interpretation of your observations is skewed. All the while you are questioning others' motives, you also need to be examining yours.

Combining personality types, body language, the spoken word, and the way you form perceptions of yourself and others will give you the bigger picture—a more well-rounded view of our intentional and unintentional communications. Knowing what you know now, you can analyze others with confidence and assurance that the things observed and heard are indicative of the meanings you have attributed to them.

As you learn about how to read one's body language and listen for the verbal clues that identify one's true motives, you can attach your perceptions of the person or situation without the concerns that you have misjudged or misread their meaning. Now it's time to look at the incredible signals and signs we send out every day without being conscious of how they help others to form their perceptions of us.

Chapter 3: Body Language Speaks Volumes

Some people are naturals at reading others, but they couldn't tell you how they know what they know. That's because they are intuitively reading others' body language, but they don't have the knowledge to define why they are such good communicators. More than 70 percent of the messages we send and receive are through non-verbal language. Not only are the greatest percent of our messages non-verbal, but that non-verbal language is more honest and genuine than the words we speak. Our bodies don't sugar coat the message; we just respond and react without being conscious of doing so.

If people are saying one thing but their body language is delivering a different message, put more stock in what you see than what you hear. However, to make sure you are reading the person correctly, let's discuss all the different nonverbal messages we send. We'll cover the nonverbal signals and what they might mean, but keep in mind that different cultures and countries might attach a different meaning to your body language. When you're confused about the nonverbal message that another is sending, then listen to the words and take the signals in context with the phrases they use.

Another way to determine the message is through the tone, pitch, and volume of another's voice. It gives truth to that saying, "It's not what you said but how you said it." When all these things are examined during your analysis of others, you'll find clarity in the message. While we're at it, there is one more thing—pay attention to the other person's required personal space. If you are questioning whether the message they are sending is positive, negative, or benevolent, step inside their personal space and be aware of their reaction. Their feelings will then be quite pronounced. If the message was meant to be off-putting, they will immediately step back or adopt a space-claiming stance that will let you know their feelings in no uncertain terms.

Facial Expressions, Features, and Head Movement

- Playing with Hair and Moving the Head

  If someone slides their fingers through their hair at the temples and tosses their head back, this is an indication they might be flirting with you. On the other hand, if they are running their fingers through their hair from their forehead through the top of their crown, that is a sign they are confused or frustrated. Tilting the head and twirling the hair is also a flirtatious mannerism, indicating interest combined with a little nervous tension.

  When people nod their heads, it matters how many times they do so before stopping. For example, public speakers who are attentive to their audiences know that three nods mean interest and attentiveness. However, if you observe a group of people conversing, you'll notice the person who nods their head only once is eager to leave and will probably be the next one to make a quick exit.

  If someone is interested in what you're saying, they will often tilt their head in your direction. They could be showing curiosity or questioning what you are saying when they bring one ear closer to make sure they are getting every detail of the conversation.

- Eye Movement

  People usually blink six or seven times a minute, but those who are stressed blink quite a bit more. If someone covers their eyes with their hands, excessively rubs their eyes, or closes their eyes, they could be hiding something or feel threatened. When the eyes are shifty or rapidly moving from one person to another, it reflects some scattered thoughts that are going on in their heads. If there is a flickering interest between two people when this is happening, then it can also be a way for people to prevent detection as they were checking out the other.

  If someone has a habit of not making eye contact or looking down as they speak, it can show shyness or can also be a cry for empathy. They are waiting for you to ask what's wrong and open the way for them to share their feelings. Investigators have come to realize that a sustained glance from a person who denies involvement in a crime, may mean they are lying and trying to over-compensate by looking them straight in the eyes for a long time to show they're telling the truth.

If you have posed a question and the person you asked looks upward, they are most likely trying to picture something they saw. On the other hand, if they look to the side toward their ear, they could be trying to recall a message they heard. If they look downward after your question, they are connecting your question with something negative and trying to find a way to avoid answering or revealing their feelings about the matter.

- Eyebrow Movement
If individuals raise their eyebrows, it usually means the person is curious about or interested in your conversation. A quick popup of one eyebrow could be a flirtation, and if the eyebrow is raised a bit longer, it often means that the other person doesn't quite buy into what you say.

If the brows furrow, you can almost bet that person is having second thoughts about what is being done or said. It most likely indicates a negative emotion like fear or confusion, so it might be time for you to back off a bit.

- Lips
Of course, a smile sends a universal message, if it is truly a smile. We've all been at the other end of a fake smile, which is one that doesn't travel all the way to the eyes and make them wrinkle in agreement. We call those "Red Carpet" smiles. They are Hollywood smiles given by people who are trying to be friendly to their fans but just want to get inside, sit down, and make it through the night.
Individuals who plaster a smile on their face almost all the time, are usually nervous. If it's in the workplace, they could feel out-of-their-depth or incompetent. There's a good chance that foreigners who smile a lot don't understand a blasted thing, so they just smile and nod.

Another thing people do with their lips is to suck on them and bite them. Sucking or biting the lip is a reaction by those who need to settle themselves down. Like a newborn, the action soothes them and offers a bit of comfort in a stressful situation. If one clamps down on their lips or purses them, it can mean frustration or anger.

Body and Limb Movements

- Body Positions

  If there is a group of people standing and talking and one or more people open their bodies to you, that is an invitation to join the conversation. If they just turn their head, you might want to choose another group. You will know if you have captured the attentions of a love interest because he or she will turn slightly toward you and point their feet in your direction, to indicate they are interested in finding out what makes you tick. If you step into the group and the person beside you touches your shoulder or arm, this is a direct ploy to show you they are interested in exploring the relationship a bit further.

  When you step into the group, if the person beside you leans into you, they genuinely like you. If their head retracts backward, perhaps something you said surprised or offended them. If they physically lean away from you, they've already made up their mind that they're not going to listen to or like you. If they turn their head in the opposite direction and follow it with their shoulder, you just got the cold shoulder. So, forget about it!

- Standing Positions

  If someone is standing with legs about shoulder width apart, it often is a sign of dominance and determination, as if they needed to stand their ground against something or prove a point. If they stand with legs together, front forward, they will hear you out, but you need to make your point quickly. When the person you are speaking with is standing and shifting their weight from side-to-side or front-to-back, it might indicate several things. They could be bored, or they are anxious and need to sooth themselves with this rocking sort of movement. To determine their feelings, it is necessary to look further at what they are doing with their arms as well.

- Arm Positions

Don't assume that crossed arms always mean that the other person is upset. Not so! Some people will stand or sit with their arms crossed because it is just a comfortable position. You can distinguish the other's emotions by looking further at their facial expression. If they have furrowed eyebrows, their mouth pursed, and their arms crossed, chances are they are angry or upset about something. Crossed arms can also be a sign of protection or a closed attitude to the ideas you are presenting.

If someone is talking with their arms flopping around, it can mean they are excited and agreeable, or it can say that they are out of control. Again, you'll need to couple your observations with other nonverbal messages to be sure. Typically, people who are overly animated are less believable and have less control over their emotions, as well as having a lack of power. They flail their arms to gain attention as if to say "I'm talking now, so would somebody please listen to me?"

- Leg and Foot Positions

  People whose toes turn inward could be closing themselves off to your comments, or they could just be pigeon-toed. To determine if there is a physiological issue that causes their toes to point it, you might need more background information. Don't rush to judgment, just wait, observe more body language, and listen to their words. Some people who began turning in their toes because they were insecure or awkward, might have created a habit that they find difficult to break. The only message they are sending is one that says; I have a physical issue that is impacting my body language.

- Sitting Positions

  If a person is spread out all over your couch, they have a feeling of self-importance. On the other hand, they probably have a good deal of confidence as well. Legs open, leaning forward with elbows on knees shows an in-charge attitude that is still open to hearing what you have to say.

  If a person is sitting next to you and crosses their legs at the knee, pointing their foot toward you, they are giving you permission to approach them. If, however, they are sitting next to you and angle their body in the opposite direction, you're probably not going to engage or connect with him or her. If that same person is fidgeting, quickly moving their ankle or foot, they are looking for a way out. Excuse yourself; both of you will probably feel more comfortable.

- Hands

When people sit on their hands, and the temperatures aren't below freezing, it could be an indication that they are deceitful—trying to hide something from you. If they walk with their hands in their pockets or behind their back, they might be relaying information, but you're not getting the full picture because they are withholding information. When you look at one's fingers and see bitten nails or chewed cuticles, you can bet that is a nervous person with low self-esteem. Or else they have put themselves in a situation that they find extremely uncomfortable.

When someone holds their hands like a church steeple and presses them to their lips, they have something important to add to the conversation but are trying to decide how to present their information. They are self-assured and will contribute when the time is right. These are the thinkers, the analytical types.

If the person is rubbing their legs with open palms pressed down, they are feeling vulnerable or uncomfortable with your nearness or your conversation. If nothing is said, don't think you are not sending a message that is perhaps louder than any words. Examine your body language and see what message you are sending to them that could be creating this reaction.

- Walking

People who advance with rather large strides are purposeful and perceived as important and competent. People think those who walk with a little bounce in their step most likely have a positive nature. And those who walk hunched over with shoulders down—well, that kind of speaks for itself, doesn't it? They are probably prone to depression and wrapped a bit too tight.

What Does One's Voice Say About Them?

There are four indicators of the quality of one's voice. They are one's intonation, volume, pitch, and rate of speech. If the voice is monotone and rather flat, they are probably bored or boring. The lack of animation in the voice could also indicate the speaker is tired. If the person's voice sounds clear and concise, they most usually are confident and powerful, more like the Leader Personality Type. If the volume is quiet or soft, the person is thought to be shy, or it could even mean they have a secret they don't want to share.

The rate of speech is also quite important when analyzing others, especially if you are attempting to mirror them to increase the chances of connectivity. For example, Leader Personality Types will usually speak fast and loud, and you need to match their volume and rate. Identifiers often speak slower than Leaders, and their pitch is more soothing than the dominant personality type. The voice can be a strong descriptive element of the individual's personality type.

By now, you have probably caught on that every movement has a message. Verify the meaning of some of the nonverbal languages by other things, such as one's words, voice, facial expressions, and gestures. To discover one's real message, you must become a student of human behavior, studying the other's movements, speech pattern, attitude, words, gestures, and expressions to analyze people successfully.

You've been introduced to the nonverbal language and the four main personality types, and to how you form accurate perceptions, but all these things are not separate from one another. They all blend to create effective communications. In the next chapter, you'll be asked to read some scenarios and identify the personality types, nonverbal indicators, and interpret the intended message.

Chapter 4: Interpreting and Responding to the Message

You've already learned how to analyze nonverbal language, but the key to excellent communications is knowing how to interpret and respond to the messages others send so that you can connect with them on a much more effective level. Wouldn't it be wonderful not to wonder what a person is thinking? Instead of questioning whether people are agreeable or accepting of your suggestions or opinions, you can use all the strategies you have learned in this book to look beyond the spoken word and read the hidden feelings people might be entertaining.

Some personality types are naturally more suited to one another, while others trigger feelings of annoyance and impatience, depending upon their key traits and character preferences. By examining each personality type a bit further, you'll gain some insight into why you instantly hit it off with some people and others just rub you the wrong way.

Leaders with Other Leaders

Partnering two Leader Personality Types is like putting two alpha dogs together in the same arena. Each one fights to lead, with nobody left to follow through and complete the task. With such competitive natures, Leaders struggle with one another to manipulate and control their environment. They are both sure their strategies and methodologies are the best, and compromise is not one of their strengths. For these reasons, placing two Leaders on a project can create unnecessary power plays, unless one's secondary personality type is a Fraternizer or Identifier.

When the relationship is personal, a coupling of two Leaders can be all work and no fun. If each is career-minded individuals, your lives will most likely not revolve around each other, but be centered on work-related events and projects. It is common when two career professionals hook up, for a while they will be quite intrigued by one another's focus and business acumen. However, as the relationship matures, the Leaders will tend to be more attentive to work-related issues, and their personal relationships suffer. If you are a Leader involved with another Leader Personality Type, you'll need to challenge one another on a personal level to keep the fires burning. Compete in a mutually enjoyed sport, or find a thrill-seeking, competitive hobby that interest both of you. It's necessary to be involved in one another's home life as well as your business endeavors.

Leaders with Perceivers

Leaders usually work well with Perceiver Personality Types because they are organizers and analytical thinkers, and their quiet, unemotional demeanor typically satisfies the Leader's goal-driven manner. The Perceiver doesn't challenge the Leader for "top dog" position because he or she doesn't enjoy being the center of attention. The downside to partnering a Leader with a Perceiver is that the professional or personal relationship can be cold and rather unexciting unless there are some Fraternizer traits in one or the other's personality.

Leaders with Fraternizers or Identifiers

If the Fraternizers or Identifiers have some secondary Perceiver or Leader traits, they will do well when relating to people who are almost all Leader types. However, if the Fraternizer or Identifier is strong in their personality traits, their empathetic and emotional behaviors will often grate on the Leader's last nerve. What Fraternizers and Identifiers need to do when communicating with a Leader or Perceiver Types is to learn to curb their feelings and reign in their emotions when interacting with these strong personalities.

The two personality types that are usually not good to put together are Leader to Leader and Fraternizer to Fraternizer, and here's why. As we said before, two Leaders will fight for the controlling position. Examining the Fraternizers, they too are competitive, and they will experience a struggle unique to their type. Fraternizers will almost always try to one-up each other, challenging one another to a more dangerous sport or a project that requires greater and greater risks. Or, Fraternizers will turn everything into such fun that there will be no work accomplished. So, let's examine how to respond best to each personality type.

Communicating with an Identifier

Avoid getting too emotional when talking with an Identifier Personality Type. Since they are rather indecisive, you'll need to continually pull them back to the task at hand and discuss the decision to make and its' probably outcome. Identifiers enjoy talking about feelings, and they will be sensitive to yours. While this is good in a personal relationship, in the office it can be distracting.

If the Identifier is your direct report, their open-door policy will enable others to frequently interrupt your time with them, creating difficulties when trying to get them to stay on task. So, be patient; your frustration will not change their policies; it will only serve to make you look grumpy and cynical. After their interruptions, they'll be tempted to discuss the other person's problems with you, which will take you further down the rabbit hole. So, count on your meetings with Identifiers taking longer and achieving less.

There is almost always delays in projects as well. The Identifier will want you to check with other team members to see how they feel about any new ideas or changes, no matter how seemingly insignificant. Or, they will insist on discussing this issue in another meeting with more managers and team members. If you aren't careful, beginning a project can take a month of meetings.

In your personal relationships, Identifiers can be a bit moody and overly sensitive. If you are a Leader personality involved with a significant other who is an Identifier, you need to get comfortable with a relationship that is emotionally demanding. Also, your need to stay focused and move forward may make them feel as though they are not being heard or valued. As a Leader, you will need to slow down and allow the Identifier to fulfill his or her need to nurture and comfort. You won't be allowed to hide away when you're sick, and too many evenings spent working at the office is going to create some emotional outbursts.

Communicating with a Perceiver

Being in a personal relationship with a Perceiver Personality Type can be a guessing game. They don't like to share their feelings, and they can be a bit stand-offish, so if you are an Identifier that needs more reassurance, just know that you're not going to get it from the Perceiver. They might have deep feelings for you, but sharing those feelings is a challenge for them.

On the other hand, if you show too many emotions in the relationship, they'll be confused and draw further back into their comfortable, quiet shell of self-protection. Perceivers can also be rather stubborn and set in their ways, so getting them to change is like pulling teeth. If you do expect change, make sure you give them plenty of time to think things through and avoid popping any surprises on them, no matter how pleasant you think it will be for them to experience the change.

For example, Laurie decided it would be a great birthday present to replace her husband, Al's football chair. It was embarrassingly worn, and the springs were giving way, so she felt he would be much more comfortable watching his favorite programs in a nice, cushy, new recliner. As a surprise, Laurie had the new chair delivered while Al was at work, and they took the tattered one away. She didn't quite get the reaction she was hoping for when Al returned from work. Although he has never complained much about his old chair, Al has merely changed his favorite seating area to a corner of the couch.

Al might have liked the idea of having a new chair had Laurie not surprised him with the idea and had his old one hauled away before he was ready for the change. He needed time to adjust to the idea that another chair could be just as comfortable, and he could have gone to the store, sat in a gazillion chairs, then slowly made his mind up to purchase the first one in which he plopped. However, without having the opportunity to think it over, look at the chairs to decide which one best suited him, and then compare prices and warranties, Al was not thrilled with Laurie's birthday present.

Communicating with a Fraternizer

Fraternizer Personality Types can get along with almost anyone, but some personality types will eventually grow weary of their tired jokes and constant need for entertainment. Also, a Perceiver will not appreciate the spontaneous spending that many Fraternizers practice. A died-in-the-wool Fraternizer with few secondary personality traits that are more grounded is often too immature and impulsive for a Leader of Perceiver in their personal relationships.

In the workplace, Fraternizers are often perceived as party people and not taken seriously. No matter how intelligent, many Fraternizers are not promoted to their potential because they allow their fun-loving spirit too much free reign in the workplace. Fraternizers usually don't make good quarterly budget planners because they spend too freely and are too rash when it comes to decision-making. If you work with a Fraternizer, you will need to keep them focused and grounded to achieve success with projects in which you are both involved.

Examining Some Personal Scenarios

Think of a co-working with whom you are currently experiencing some challenges when communicating with him or her. Now review the following questions to determine the other person's personality type and what you can do to create a more positive working relationship.

- What is your subject's dominant personality type? How do you know this?
- What is your dominant personality type?
- What does this person do that annoys you? Analyze these behaviors to see if this is a trait of their personality type?
- What do you think you are doing that annoys him or her?
- Is this your imagination, or are you reading their non-verbal language?
- What was the last challenge you experienced with him or her?
- Based on his or her personality type, how could you have responded better to create a more positive outcome?
- Knowing what you know now, how will you communicate with this person in the future to create a better relationship?

Now, think of a personal relationship you would like to improve and ask yourself the same questions. When you determine the other's personality type, make sure you verify your beliefs by observing their behaviors, listening to their words, and analyzing the body language they are displaying around you. Ask yourself if you are too sensitive because of your personality type, or if you really are having serious communication issues with this person.

If you cannot answer the questions about people who challenge you, then keep reading. The next chapter will deal with Three Key Elements to Connectivity, which will give you some useful tools to help you to analyze others accurately.

Chapter 5: Three Key Elements to Connectivity

There are three critical key elements to one's ability to successfully connect with others: mindful observation, listening with intent, and effective feedback.

Connecting with Others Through Mindful Observation

So, what is meant by mindful observation? Like most of us, you observe people and your surroundings all the time, but what do you take away from the things you see? How do you apply what you see to help you monitor and adjust your behaviors and beliefs? The reality is, most people use very little of what they see to improve their communications. If they are more aware than most, they might see that what they are saying is not being well received by their audience. Consequently, they just stop communicating. Most people make very few adjustments to improve their communications. Instead, they only pass the baton to the next person in the conversation who is eager to participate.

In most instances, there is no monitoring and adjusting of verbal and non-verbal language because many individuals have never learned how to analyze people and adjust their communication style to be more accommodating to that person's personality type. The powers of observation can only help when people put what they see to work and create a more active exchange of information.

To improve your observation skills, you need to work like a dog! You heard—just like a dog. Dogs have amazing observation skills. In fact, trainers say that the best way to teach a dog to do the trick is by letting them see another dog perform it and receive a reward. A dog's observation skills are so keen that they learn better by watching than by verbal commands. Who's to say the same thing isn't so for humans?

Marsha's dog is so observant, Hannah knows what she'll be doing that day based on the things she observes her owner doing. For example, if Marsha pulls out her running shoes, Hannah knows they are going for a run. If Marsha pulls her hair back into a ponytail, Hannah suspects they are going herding and runs into the garage to wait at the car door because Marsha always wears her hair in a ponytail when she takes Hannah herding.

The problem comes when Marsha decides to pull her hair into a ponytail, and she's not taking Hannah herding. Hannah is so sure she's going herding that she begins to scratch and pester Marsha as if to ask why she pulled the switch. Hannah is relentless in her attempts to get Marsha to do as she wants, confident they'll be leaving soon. Hannah's so sure of her ability to read her owner that she will stand at the garage door for almost an hour waiting for Marsha's approach. The problem is, although Hannah read all the signs, she didn't know that the same sign could have several meanings.

The reason I tell this story is to warn you that sometimes you can have excellent observation skills and yet with this one person this one time, they don't work. What you observe and attach meaning to isn't want was intended. You keep doing the same thing, and yet you aren't getting the results you want. Your communication isn't improving, and neither is your relationship. When this happens, change things. Don't assume the same thing works for all people. Try something different to get to better communications. The most important aspect to remember is that giving up gets you nowhere.

Sometimes you just need to observe a little longer or a bit more. Don't' just see the person as they communicate with you, watch how they communicate with others. Watch how others react to them. If this is a person with whom you have issues, watch their body language around those you know they like. Listen to their voice as they speak with others with whom they communicate well. Then observe how that other person responds to the one with whom you have issues. How does their voice sound? What is their body language saying? How are they standing or sitting that is different from the way you respond? For complicated relationships, surface observations just aren't enough.

You must be mindful of your goal as you observe your subject. What is it you want from the relationship? Being aware means you can't always focus on all things going on around them, but you need to choose just one or two things to observe for a while until you have a greater understanding of what they are saying with that gesture or expression. Once you know that, then move on to something else. Being mindful in your observations means you are determined to resolve the situation and improve the communications with that person.

Listening with Intent

Just as people observe others every day, they also hear them as well. The downside is you can hear someone, but if you are listening with a specific intent, you won't know what to do with what you hear. For instance, you can hear someone speaking, but if you are not listening with the intent to distinguish the person's rate of speech when they are talking or the volume of which they speak with a plan to identify their personality type, then you hear only part of the message.

When listening with intent, you don't interrupt, you don't plan what you're going to say next while the other is still talking, and you don't speak over that person. In fact, you don't speak at all; you listen, and you listen with the intent of discovering the meaning behind the words and between the lines.

Giving Effective Feedback

Sometimes providing effective feedback is nothing more than mimicking a person's rate or volume of speech. At other times, useful feedback means adopting an open, relaxed stance to reflect what you would like to see the other person do as well. Then there are times effective feedback means adjusting your personality traits a bit so that you don't make the other person uncomfortable or annoyed. If your message is garbled because your body language, gestures, and expressions are different from your words, then you need to bring clarity to the conversation by providing congruent feedback.

Of course, there are times where you don't want people to read what you are thinking, and in that case, effective feedback will be that which masks the way you feel. It is not about hiding your feelings, but more liked controlling them. It's not beneficial to you or anyone else if you always reveal every single thought and feeling. There are times you need to bury your emotions a bit so that your communications don't expose you or put you in a vulnerable position. In these cases, effective feedback is NOT revealing what you don't want another to know.

Practice these three key elements to connectivity and others will not only feel connected to you, but they will be more supportive of your ideas and suggestions. It's a way to get what you want without emotional outbursts and unreasonable demands. You get your way because you are an outstanding communicator. You get the support of others because they like you and because you GET them. You achieve success in your personal and professional life because you connect with others and they with you, and all because of the few strategies you've learned from these pages. Don't look now, but you've just practiced the three key elements to connectivity: mindful observation, listening with intent, and providing effective feedback.

Chapter 6: The Beauty of Successfully Analyzing Others

What a thrill it is to learn to analyze others and stop the anxiety of wondering how someone feels about you or what they think of your ideas or suggestions. Learning how to read someone's body language is as exciting as learning how to understand the author's meaning in a book or interpret a foreign language. What will help you to continue practicing and improving your analytical skills is to understand that you don't become an expert at reading others overnight. It takes time, practice, and a willingness to adopt good listening and observation skills to become an exceptional communicator.

There are tremendous payoffs that come from successfully analyzing others. The better you get, the more friends you'll have because people gravitate to those they like. The more you practice the strategies learned in this book, the better you'll get at reading people and adjusting your behaviors and language to match others. Soon analyzing one's body language and gestures will become second nature to you, and you'll wonder why you failed to notice the distinctive messages the body sends long before now.

Many aspects of your life will improve along with your communications. You'll have opportunities offered, and doors opened that were previously always out of reach. You'll see the world differently because the world will see you differently as well. Your confidence and self-esteem will raise with your increased ability to accurately analyze others. People will gain a new appreciation of you, and you'll be asked to participate in work projects or on teams whose members before may not have chosen you as a player.

There's magic in excellent communications, and that magic is making meaningful, long-lasting relationships. You'll look back on those people who you once considered the "beautiful" people and suddenly realize that you have joined their ranks. It may sound far-fetched, but our entire lives revolve around our ability to connect with others by speaking their language, by understanding the message they are sending, and by offering feedback that supports and enhances others.

One of the best feelings you can create in another person is that they are better off for having known you, for having kept company with you, and that's what learning to analyze people can do. People will leave your presence feeling good about spending time with you. You will leave the company of others without concern that your message wasn't understood or appreciated. Analyzing others is a work of art—a work of beauty—a treasure of information to be studied, enjoyed and shared.

Conclusion: Congratulations on Your Read

Thank you so much for purchasing this book!

I hope reading *How to Analyze People: How to Master Reading Anyone Instantly Using Body Language, Human Psychology, and Personality Types* will help you to improve your personal and professional communications significantly.

The next step is to put these strategies to work in your life to create great relationships.

Thank you and good luck on your new skills of analyzing people.

Book #3
Manipulation

The Definitive Guide to Understanding Manipulation, Mind Control and NLP

Introduction

I want to thank you and congratulate you for purchasing the book, *"Manipulation: The Definitive Guide to Understanding Manipulation, Mind Control, and NLP"*.

There are always instances, throughout life, where you can't get exactly what you desire, but you never need to settle for being disappointed. Instead, you can learn about manipulation and mind control, how to use it on others with NLP techniques, and spot when others are using it on you. Most people believe that manipulation is a negative thing, and the concept generally gets a bad rap, but that all depends on what type of manipulation you're using. In this book, we will go over the following:

- **Defining Manipulation:** As mentioned above, there is a lot of misunderstanding surrounding this word, what it means, how it's used, and more. In this guide, you will learn what you need to know about the concept of manipulation and general persuasion and influence.

- **The Benefits of Using it Right, and How to do that:** Manipulation can be used in a positive way that benefits all parties involved, but this is something you have to learn about to master.

- **How to Spot and Avoid Negative Manipulation:** If you aren't aware of what it looks like to be manipulated by others, it's almost certain that it will happen to you, which could be dangerous. Leaving yourself upon to the whim of whoever wishes to manipulate you could have long lasting harmful effects

Thanks again for purchasing this book, I hope you enjoy it!

Chapter 1: What is Manipulation and How does it Work?

Manipulation exists in everyone's life on the planet. Within the human mind, a few different groups of shortcuts exist that leave us vulnerable to manipulation, and there are countless combinations and variations of these. Many people are even willing to put their lives on the line for them, which is no exaggeration. Some people will pick a job they hate, drink poison, or risk their lives in war. They might even get into an accident on the street completely unaware that they are following through actions of a story they read in the paper the day before. Most importantly, they would be spending money and time.

What is Manipulation?

Manipulation is the influence a person uses to try to alter the perceptions or behaviors of others. Often, it's done through underhanded, deceptive, or abusive techniques, but not always. In some people's opinions, when a manipulator advances their own interests using these techniques, without consideration for the needs of others, the methods are exploitative.

- **Negative Manipulation:** This is when you intentionally withhold information from someone to get what you want, play up your own emotions in a false way to persuade someone, or otherwise threaten them indirectly for selfish reasons. Negative manipulation has harmed countless people in the world. Being under the negative manipulation of another person can make you feel like you're crazy, or act in ways that you would normally never act. We will cover this in more detail in later chapters.

  This method of manipulation relies on hidden agendas, ulterior motives, and attempts to force others to give into your will. Although the manipulator looks in control and strong on the surface, they often feel very insecure on the inside; otherwise they wouldn't need to engage in such behaviors. The actions of these people (such as disregarding and exploiting the rights of other people) are a signal of a lack of health, on a mental level. In fact, people who engage in these behaviors have a hard time finding and keeping positive relationships with others.

- **Positive (or Ethical) Manipulation:** Also known as persuasion or influence, this is when you convince someone to come around to your ways of thinking or acting, but in a way that also benefits them. This has a positive, rather than harmful, effect. There are a few clear distinctions between negative and positive manipulation, and it's important to make sure you know the difference. Everyone uses positive manipulation and influence to further our own goals with other people, which is perfectly fine and normal. This method of manipulation acknowledges the boundaries and rights of others, and uses honest and direct communication.

This method of manipulation is a simple way to function efficiently and effectively in your environment, and to benefit and make use of the social order that exists in our world. It recognizes that other people have a basic integrity, and a choice of whether or not to follow through with your persuasion attempts. In essence, this acknowledges that each person should be autonomous and acknowledges a baseline of human respect between you and others. We are all social creatures who need each other, in one way or another.

What is NLP and How does it Relate to this?

NLP (or Neuro-Linguistic Programming) is a study that focuses on the elements that allow us to experience the world. These elements are programming, language, and the neurology of our brains. Our neurological systems control the way our physical bodies work, language regulates the way we communicate with the world and other people, and the programming we go through in life decides what our models of reality will look like. All of this determines who we will be, what we will think like, what our habits will be, and what type of lives we will lead. We will discuss, in more detail, NLP techniques in a later chapter of this book.

Being aware of these definitions allows you to use knowledge to better your life. When you are aware of what methods can be used to influence you, suddenly you are empowered to make choices about what does. This book will teach you how to recognize manipulation methods being used today, along with methods for resisting them. You will also learn about using the ingrained mental shortcuts we all have to persuade, manipulate, and influence others. Let's look at something we are all familiar with, advertising, to illustrate how this works.

Manipulation in Advertising vs. Personal Manipulation:

How exactly is manipulation in advertising done? Advertisers utilize many different techniques for manipulating customers or potential consumers. These include appeals to emotions and feelings, ads that are disguised as other forms of entertainment, and ads that appeal to insecurities or fears. As these strategies become more and more sophisticated and complex, consumers can recognize and resist the manipulative or deceptive tactics by learning more about how they work. In addition to this, you can apply this knowledge the techniques that people use to manipulate each other. Let's look at some of the manipulation techniques of advertising, to get a better understanding of this subject:

- **Emotional Reactions:** Advertisers know that emotions are a great way to elicit specific feelings in people, and they use this to their advantage. Advertisers often play up or emphasize the feelings that products will bring you, rather than actual characteristics or qualities of the products. In fact, a lot of ads aim to elicit a feeling response that distracts customers from considering the functionality or value of the product. They might show specific scenarios that consumers can remember or relate to in some other way, like your first child's birth, or a date. This increases the feeling response and engagement, emotionally, that viewers will feel with that product.

    This same technique is used in interpersonal manipulation. For example, a friend or significant other who is trying to convince you to do something you don't want to do might try to encourage you by telling you it will be fun, or even bringing up past memories to elicit a feeling response in you. Some may also use fear tactics to elicit a negative emotion, or a fear of a negative emotion in others to get them to do what they want. This is, for example, used often by parents who threaten their children with being punished unless they follow through on orders.

- **Ads Disguised as Simple Entertainment:** It becomes more and more common that ads disguise themselves as simple entertainment, providing depictions of humorous or relatable narratives to attract consumers. Skillful or clever screen writing, cute animal mascots, and unique or memorable strategies all help to make customers feel more engaged, and thus likelier to remember the product being advertised. Some ads will even show the most outrageous scenarios they can invent to make this happen. Companies that sell products that are unhealthy, like candy or beer, tend to utilize humor techniques to distract viewers from detrimental or negative factors of products.

This type of technique used in advertising can be compared to interpersonal manipulation tactics which misrepresent true intentions. For example. Someone who is manipulating you might tell you that their intentions are something completely different than they really are. They might pretend to only wish to entertain or please you, when they truly have ulterior motives. They might also use flattery or other false narratives to further their own personal agenda.

- **Using Fear and Insecurity:** Advertisers are famous for preying on the insecurities of consumers. For example, TV commercials may depict a character that they wish to portray as "unattractive" or lesser than others by focusing on a particular "flaw", such as baldness, or yellowing teeth. They then appear to offer the magical solution to the problem by attempting to sell you their product. Another example of using fear as an ad tactic is advertising for soap or other cleaning products during times when sickness is prevalent. Many times, their products don't actually help combat the sickness at all.

An example of this tactic being used in interpersonal relations is in romantic relationships. Perhaps one person is ready to break up and move on, but the other is afraid to live without them. Instead of respecting the person's choice to leave and move on with their life, they try to appeal to that person's insecurities by insinuating that they will never find someone as good. Fear is a perfect example of a negative manipulation tactic that is good to guard yourself against. We will show you how to do that later on in the book.

The Rule of Reciprocation, a Common Technique:

One common and famous technique for manipulating others using automatic or subconscious behavior, is called the rule of reciprocation. The basic idea behind this "rule" is that if someone else does something nice for you, you should do something for them in return. This is something we are all taught from childhood, either directly or indirectly, and is so ingrained that nearly nobody questions it. This tactic is used often to manipulate others.

- **Sample Counters:** Think about samples given out at grocery stores. The idea behind them is that if someone gives you a taste of something at no cost, your mind will see it as a favor and make you more likely to purchase their product. Instead of having people paid to walk around and ask people if they would like to buy something, they have people giving out free stuff, which makes others more obligated to listen to what the sales person has to say.

- **Door to Door Fundraisers:** Another area this tactic is used in is fundraising efforts. When someone goes door to door to try to collect donations from people, they are a lot more likely to get someone to listen to what they have to say (and therefore, at times, donate) if they offer something first. Simple techniques like this can make donations multiply and sky rocket, due to basic psychology manipulation techniques.

This rule applies to favors big and small and you don't necessarily feel obligated to return the same amount of "good" or favor back to someone who has done something for you. In fact, you can do someone a tiny favor, and then ask them for something big, and the trick still has an effect. For example, you could offer to help someone carry groceries in from their car, or mention that you have dedicated hours of your life to them (implying that they now owe you big.) Of course, this type of manipulation can be used for good aims, such as getting your child to do their schoolwork or study for a test, convincing your sick mother to go to the doctor, or getting your manager to give you a raise. These techniques can be used to discover the true reason behind issues going on at work or in the family, and help people move past harmful habits they are stuck in.

Ways of using these Techniques in Everyday Life:

There are important distinctions between NLP methods and the techniques listed above. A quality NLP method benefits people and incorporates mental tricks like the one mentioned above (reciprocity). However, you don't have to be aware of NLP or hypnosis methods to use manipulation techniques.

- **The Hypnotist Metaphor:** You might find it useful to think about the following metaphor. Envision being a hypnotist who must convince a patient or subject to stop moving and be completely still. You have to get them to look forward and ignore all noises besides your instructions. You could use techniques for building rapport, or trance techniques, which may or may not actually work.

- **Considering the Person:** It's important, when learning about or trying to partake in manipulation, to know your subject. If the person you are trying to get to focus, for example, has been employed by the military at one point, wearing official general clothes from their army and calling out "Attention!" will do the trick. Conditioning is something that is often with us for life, whether we are aware of it or not. This means that you are not creating new responses or reactions in the person, but simply calling upon something that already exists within them.

How are Mental Shortcuts related to Manipulation?

It's obvious why these behaviors are thought of as automatic reactions, but how are mental shortcuts related? In the language of NLP, this could be called distortion, deletion, or generalization, but we are going to keep it simple for now. Let's start with how human beings think and relate to the world, something everyone has firsthand experience with.

- **Shortcuts for Survival:** Our world is complicated and we are constantly surrounded by new stimuli. It's impossible for humans to constantly think about every factor that is needed, which is why certain processes are automated. Perhaps we would still survive without this, but it would be extremely inefficient. Think, for example, about operating your car. Can you recall when you first started driving, and the way you needed to pay close attention to every single part of the process? But now, it's simply automatic. This is done by utilizing mental shortcuts.

Rather than having to stop and agonizingly consider every angle of every sign or light, you already know what to do instinctively due to repetition. Think now about reading information or news on the internet. How do you figure out whether stories you're reading are true or false? You aren't going to thoroughly research every article every time. Instead, you apply mental shortcuts to find your answer and opinion.

- **How these Shortcuts leave us Vulnerable:** This part is important. Not everyone realizes that they are employing these mental shortcuts throughout the day. They simply happen automatically, without much thought, after all that's the point of them, right? But this automated process of thinking and acting can leave us vulnerable to others who wish to manipulate these tendencies. Although we need these automatic processes and shortcuts for survival, to make decisions quickly with minimal thought and effort, they are often used against us.

    The examples above given of advertising manipulation tactics are a depiction of this at work, as are the tactics used by politicians during speeches. Everyone knows the terms "clearance" and "sale." When signs exclaiming either one of these are placed out front of a store, people know to expect good deals and bargains on their shopping trips. When we see an advert claiming that there is a limited time, great offer happening at their location, our subconscious minds pick up on this.

These mental shortcuts are all around us and a very important part of our lives. Statistics prove that a guy who is better looking will receive a less harsh conviction or sentence in court. Studies have shown that American citizens are far more likely to vote for someone who looks friendly and paternal, because of our mental associations of seeing people like this as more trustworthy. Salespeople will be more successful in their sales if they simply present their items in a certain way. We cannot control our own automatic thought processes and conditioning, but becoming aware of this is beneficial for many reasons.

Chapter 2: The Benefits of Learning about this Skill

Learning about manipulation, both in its positive and negative forms, is important for any human who wishes to function in a healthy way. Using persuasion techniques from NLP studies can increase your ability to ethically manipulate others and be more influential, in general. Ethical manipulation is an important skill in life, and can be used for influencing clients, members of your family, or colleagues at work. Anyone who learns about NLP for this reason will access useful and powerful abilities to help support the process of ethical manipulation and persuasion.

The Benefits of Knowing about Persuasion and Manipulation:

Mastering these skills and the fine art of ethical manipulation will give you new opportunities for increases in your sales numbers, getting to know important or influential figures, better self-esteem, and the ability to express yourself naturally and authentically. The art of persuasion is an important part of the theory of communication, and these methods help create and foster healthy relations on a community level, along with customer and employee relations. When you are good at employing the correct use of argumentation, it will lead to raises, promotions, and influential or powerful positions. Let's look at a few more benefits to this:

- **Rapport:** One important benefit to learning about ethical manipulation is using it to build rapport with others. Rapport is what helps us feel at ease with another person, feel common ground, and look for qualities shared in common. It is necessary for all positive interactions and achieving goals that include other people. Essentially, this happens when you feel comfortable with someone, relate to them easily, and have a warm interaction with them. Rapport relies on seeing common ground between you and another person.

    It's an important aspect of persuasion and manipulation because people are a lot more likely to do favors for others, or simply agree with them, if they see that person as similar to themselves. Therefore, everyone who knows how to ethically persuade others is aware of building rapport. In this book, we will give you a few methods for doing this with many different types of people. No matter how different the person seems from you, it's possible to find common ground and build rapport if you simply know how.

- **Seeing the Needs and Wants of Others:** When you are effective at persuading other people, or knowing how to read signs of them trying to persuade, you catch a glimpse into what they find the most important. In this way, you can understand humanity on a deeper level, and use this information to get ahead in life. When you recognize others' wants and needs, not only do you better understand them as an individual, but you can become closer. This is what separates positive and negative manipulation.

- **Effective Communication:** Rapport-building and recognizing the needs of others are foundations that can lead to effective communication. Effectively communicating is useful for countless reasons, among which are conflict resolution, getting ahead in your career, and resolving conflicts on a professional and personal level. Let's look at the example of building healthy relations with employees from your work. Talking to them about benefit decreases, or impending layoffs, along with other unpleasant company decisions, requires a certain level of savvy that can be gained using ethical manipulation techniques.

One method for dong this relies on reaching your listeners using logic and facts. You could, for example, show that if your business doesn't close down a certain property, the rest of your businesses will have to close down. The second method relies on the fact that your listeners are paying attention mostly on an emotional plane, rather than using logic. In situations like this, appealing to empathy by illustrating examples of families who will suffer as a result of not taking action is more effective. As mentioned earlier in the book, knowing your audience is important for effectively persuading people.

- **Finding Shared Values with Anyone:** There are times, in life, when we are forced to work along with or spend time with people who seem very different from us. When you are effective at persuasion and ethical manipulation, this becomes easy. You can simply find shared values with them, no matter how different they appear to be on the surface. This allows you access to the skills of lightening tension in tough situations, or getting people to do you favors readily. People are more likely to help those who they see as similar to them, meaning that knowing how to find similarities is a must for interpersonal relations.

- **Beating Resistance:** Marketing depends entirely on the buying habits of consumers. One hard habit to beat is buyer resistance in consumers. Effectively persuading buyers means helping them to feel at ease with their choices, while simultaneously improving your sales numbers. A main factor in doing this is displaying to the buyer your understanding of the hard choice they are facing. Letting them know that you are aware of how difficult the purchase is and understand their feelings can allow them to let down their guard.

This allows the buyer to see you more as a human. They may then make a purchase that benefits them and you, as the sales person. This of course applies not just to sales, but to interpersonal situations. Empathizing with another person is a great way to get them to open up, feel more comfortable, and become decisive about important choices.

- **Expressing Yourself more Effectively:** Skills in influence and positive manipulation helps individuals to express themselves authentically. Constructing logical and sound arguments that people come to agree with creates and sustains self-assuredness and confidence. Arguments that use logic rely on facts, not just opinions. Even though a person might start with a certain idea or opinion, researching the situation or material will allow them a chance to give others important and valid data and information. Speakers who are truly powerful and influential use facts to support their arguments, and use that information to prove that they are correct.

Techniques for Persuasion and Manipulation Skills:

This book will go over many different techniques for this, but let's start with the following basics:

- **Mirroring:** This is one of the quickest ways to build rapport with someone you just met. You pay attention to their bodily movements, tone of voice, and values, and mirror them subtly. For example, if someone is standing with their arms crossed, do the same thing. If they are speaking excitedly and quickly, match their tone and pitch. This must be done in a very subtle way or it will have the opposite effect you're hoping for. The reason why this is so effective is because you can eventually have someone follow you to a conclusion or decision that you wish for them to reach.

- **Questioning:** Another technique for this is discovering what people need and want by asking questions. You do this to elicit their personal values and figure out what they think is most important in this world, then you can appeal to those values by aligning your idea, service, or product with what they find important.

- **Honesty:** This is a key difference in ethical manipulation and negative, selfish manipulation. Effective influence and persuasion rely on honesty and transparency. Real, genuine, positive persuasion makes no attempt to fool the audience, but rather gives a grouping of facts and information that the audience can consider to make the best choice. Learning the skill of effective influence using solid communication techniques can drastically improve self-esteem levels, job performance, and chances of securing positions of leadership.

Influence and persuasion should always be used for helping others, rather than hurting them. False information shouldn't be used or given, and if you have a good understanding of true ethical manipulation, it will never be necessary. There are many benefits to gain from learning about NLP, including an extreme increase in your persuasion abilities, which might be the most important social skill you could develop. Since NLP techniques are so valuable, that is what we'll be focusing on in much of this guide. This chapter was intended to illustrate how important this skill is, so hopefully you now have a fuller understanding of the subject.

Chapter 3: Manipulation and Influence Techniques

The simplest and easiest method for manipulating others, particularly American citizens, is by appealing to their feelings. Although you can use logic to help people reach a logical decision, you can also guide them in feeling particular emotions that lead to the results you want. This is the essence of manipulation. This book will cover a wide variety of techniques to use for this, but first we are going to cover some tips that get you into the right frame of mind for persuading others. Here are some techniques and tips to help you along:

- **Get a Hold of your Own Feelings First:** It can be easier to influence or ethically manipulate someone who is more on the indecisive side, but you can also persuade people with a strong resolve to consider and come over to your point of view. Being aware of your own feelings and how they come across to others is an important part of this. In order to persuade others, you have to be relatable to them, and in order to be relatable, you have to know which emotions to show, how, and when.

  For example, accessing a confident state of mind when interacting with someone makes you come across as calm and collected, meaning that others, especially indecisive people, will gladly follow your lead. Exhibiting your adventurous or authoritative qualities can be especially influential when you're around someone who is more on the shy side. The key lies in knowing which personality traits to show and when and who to do that around.

- **Become Charismatic:** Throwing tantrums and crying to get your way might work for some, but being charismatic and having people like you is a much better way to exert influence and effectively manipulate the feelings others have of you. It's also a good way to reach for mutually beneficial outcomes to your persuasion. Charm is a foundational part of this. When you are likeable in the majority of situations, reacting with strong emotions in specific situations will have more impact on others. So study up on becoming more charismatic, dress well, and make sure you treat others with respect. All of that will help you be more influential.

Being charismatic is all about getting people to feel comfortable around you. You can do this by showing that you care about them. Instead of simply talking about what you like and what you think, ask people for their input and opinions. This shows that you value them as a person and think they are worth listening to. In addition to this, make sure you make eye contact during conversations, but not too much. Essentially, you should be looking directly at someone's face for at least 60 percent of the conversation.

- **Humanize Yourself to Others:** One way to get others to trust you and open up to you more easily is to humanize yourself to them. One way to do this is to share personal information with them that is relevant and allows them to feel as though you trust them with something. When this happens, they are more likely to open up to you and allow you to influence them. This is similar to, and draws off of, the technique of reciprocation discussed in an earlier chapter of the book.

People automatically like you more when you decide to confide something in them. Depending on the situation, this will vary, so use your judgment. For example if you are trying to persuade someone to trust your advice as a veterinarian, you could share a personal anecdote about having to put your lifelong companion, Fluffy, down when you were a kid, and how it all worked out for the best. If you wish for your friend to take your advice on a breakup, relate a story about a hard time you went through that is similar in nature.

- **Positivity:** When you are attempting to persuade or ethically manipulate another person, your worst enemy is doubt. You should maintain positive relations with the person you're talking to, and never resort to attacking or negativity. Not only does this poison possible relations between you and the other person, but it makes you a very ineffective influencer. Show your best qualities to make yourself relatable and likeable.

- **Mention Advantages and Benefits:** Getting people to come around to a specific way of thinking or acting often means you must display good reasons for them to do so. Mention explicit benefits and advantages to them coming around to your opinion on the matter. If you're trying to sell something to someone, for example, list the worries that they will be free from with your product.

There are many different ways to manipulate, control, and influence the feeling response that people have to you. Realizing this is the essence of leadership and true influence. Perhaps the most important skill of all is being a likeable person. Now that we have covered some of the benefits to manipulation (when used in a positive and uplifting manner), it's time to discuss some of the negative and harmful effects that irresponsible manipulation can lead to.

Chapter 4: How to Recognize Negative Manipulation

One of the most important parts of learning about manipulation is figuring out how to protect yourself from it. Nearly everyone in this world has been manipulated negatively in some way or another, and it never feels good or nice. Everyone on this planet just wants to meet their own needs, but people who use negative manipulation use deceit and underhanded techniques for doing so, instead of honesty and an approach of mutual benefit. In essence, they don't care about your wants or needs, and only wish to serve themselves. This relies on subtly influencing another person with abusive, deceptive, or hidden tactics.

Veiled Hostility and Intimidation Tactics:

At first, it might come across as flattering, friendly, and harmless, like that person only has your best interests at heart, but that is never the case with negative manipulation. Sometimes, it's barely concealed hostility, and when someone uses these abusive techniques, they are trying to gain power over you. At times, you might not even know that you're being intimidated subconsciously. When you're used to manipulation from childhood or the past, it can be more difficult to recognize it or know what's happening because it's familiar and might even feel natural in some ways. You may feel an instinctual anger or discomfort, while the manipulator uses reasonable, ingratiating, or pleasant terms that appeal to your sympathy or guilt. This leads to you overriding your gut feelings and not knowing how to respond.

Who uses these Negative Tactics?

People in codependent relationships might have a hard time being assertive or direct, leading to the use of negative manipulation to achieve their personal goals. These types might also become victims of narcissists or sociopaths. Abusive partners might use these tactics, as well.

How to Recognize Negative Manipulation:

There are a few tactics that every manipulator uses, and these are favors and gifts, flattery, over the top apologies, fake sympathy, false concern, evasion techniques or avoidance, blackmail, making assumptions about you, playing with your mind, undermining your thoughts and feelings, bribing you, blaming you, faking innocence, making excuses, comparing, complaining, and guilt tripping. Let's look at a few of these techniques in detail:

- **Favors with "Strings Attached":** They will often utilize the technique of guilt either directly or in an implied way. They do you favors and then hold them over your head later when they want something from you.

- **Getting Power through Sympathy:** Some negative manipulators will deny agreements, conversations, or promises they made you. They might also intentionally start fights and then blame you in order to gain power by upsetting you.

- **Bribery:** Bribery is very commonly used by parents in order to get their kids to follow their instructions. For example, your parents might bribe you to go to the school they want you to attend, by buying you a new car.

- **Using Assumptions:** Negative manipulators will often make assumption aloud about you or your beliefs or intentions, and then respond to those assumptions. They will ignore what you say to the contrary as a way to justify their actions and feelings. They might even pretend as though you have agreed or decided something to effectively ignore your objections or input on the subject. For example, they will tell you how you feel, and respond to that, instead of asking you how you feel and listening.

- **Pressured Reciprocation:** We discussed the influence tactic of reciprocation, where you offer someone something small and then follow up with a larger request. This can be harmless, but when it's used with pressure or guilt, that's when it becomes a negative manipulation tactic. When you say no to their request, they will turn around and try to make themselves out to be the victim. It will be all about the manipulator and their personal issues, leading you to feel defensive.

They will then bring up past occurrences of you not fulfilling their wishes, and lay a lot of blame on you to try to get you to agree with what they want. They don't care if it hurts you at all, in fact, as long as it makes you do what they want. You get the feeling, when it comes to a negative manipulator, that there are always hidden motives or strings attached when they offer something to you or act kind.

- **False Concern or Blackmail:** This is a tactic, which relies on "well-meaning worry", that is intended to make you doubt yourself or to invalidate your choices. The negative manipulator might also use shame, threats, intimidation, or anger tactics to get you to do what they want. They may shame you to make you feel doubt and insecurity, even masking this with a false compliment. People who use blackmail might also use anger to scare you, leading you to putting aside your wants and needs to do what they want.

If this method doesn't work on you, they might switch suddenly to a more positive mood and act nice toward you. This could lead you to feel relieved and become willing to do what they ask you to do. They may also bring up shameful memories from your past and threaten to tell others about it if you don't comply with their wishes. This may lead the victim of the negative manipulation to feel fearful to say no. If they say no, they will likely experience insults from the manipulator, such as being called selfish.

- **Passive Aggressive Manipulation**: Some people, especially those who are on the shy side, use passive manipulation tactics, since most people with codependent personalities are not very assertive. They might act agreeable on the surface, telling people what they want to hear, and then break their agreements later on. Instead of responding honestly to an issue that could lead to fighting or some type of confrontation, they avoid instead, try to change the subject, or deny and blame, using rationalizations and excuses.

They are afraid to be wrong, and due to finding it difficult to raise conflict, they say yes even when they don't agree, and then follow up with complaints or guilt trips about how hard it will be to accommodate the other person. When someone confronts them, they may feel shame and have a hard time claiming responsibility for their actions. So instead, they create excuses, blame others, or try to "fix" things by apologizing, even if they don't mean it.

Even these passive tactics, which aren't as obvious as the tactics of anger or shaming, are a method for expressing hostile feelings. These could involve saying yes to a request and then "forgetting" to follow through on it, because you never wanted to in the first place.

- **Self-Pity and Criticism**: Negative manipulators might use flattery and charm, offering to do nice favors for you, help with something you need assistance with, or give you gifts in order to gain your love and acceptance. Then they will turn around and use manipulation tactics like self-pity, guilt, and criticism to get others to follow along with their desires. "Why are you always so selfish? I help you when you need it." They constantly pull the victim card.

The best way to figure out a defense against manipulation is to know who you're dealing with and going up against. Every negative manipulator has different tactics, and if they know you well, they're already aware of what triggers you. Become aware of their methods for doing this and learn to recognize it when they attempt to use them on you. Build up your self-respect and self-worth, which will be your greatest defense.

Chapter 5: How to Avoid being Manipulated

Now that we have gone over some of the methods and tactics people use to negatively manipulate others, it's time to talk about how to avoid these methods. Negative manipulation can be defined as convincing others to do whatever you desire, without offering something of value back to them. How does this phenomenon work?

- **A Threat and no Value:** If a person says, "Help me finish this project or I'm going to be angry with you," they are trying to negatively manipulate your actions. They are not actually offering anything of value to you in return. However, if a friend offers you something of value in return for a favor, that isn't negative manipulation, because you're getting something back for the effort you put in.

- **Making another Responsible for their Emotions:** Another form of manipulation is telling someone that they are responsible for how you feel and that they should feel guilty for that. For example, telling them that if they don't come to your party, you will be highly disappointed. This implies that it's their fault how you feel. However, if you offer to introduce your friend to someone they have been wanting to meet at your party, you are offering a situation that allows both of you to win.

Why do People Manipulate?

What are people's reasons for manipulating others? These can be anything from innocent and even friendly reasons to mean and selfish, but for the sake of this chapter, we're going to focus on negative and selfish manipulation.

- **Misery Likes Company:** They do it because they gain satisfaction, on an emotional level, from seeing the frustrated or otherwise negative responses of others. Certain people are so unhappy with their lives and themselves that they try to bring others down by creating problems for them.

- **It makes them feel Powerful:** Someone who is insecure and feels powerless will often try to exert power in other areas to make up for it. Getting others to do what they want gives them temporary satisfaction.

- **A Lack of Importance:** Another reason why people negatively manipulate others is because they don't think that they are important. They believe that if they simply request what they wish for, they won't get it because they don't matter enough. So instead, they try to make us feel ashamed or guilty as a consequence for not doing what they want, as a preemptive measure from disappointment.

- **They are "too Good" for some Things:** Other negative manipulators simply think that they are too good for certain tasks. They might see other people as below them, and therefore expect those people to do the tasks that they don't want to do. This could be due to laziness, or simply an inflated sense of self.

- **Not Knowing how to get Things done:** Some negative manipulators don't think that they are capable of gaining what they want, and instead operate under the assumption that they must convince and pressure others to do their bidding for them.

- **Selfishly "Helping" Others:** Other negative manipulators actually convince themselves that what they are doing will help people. This is a common idea embraced by people who think that they know better than others what is best for everyone. Due to their beliefs that they have a higher intelligence or ability, they feel satisfied doing this, and convince themselves that the people being manipulated are better off for it.

Actually, the majority of negative manipulators are not actually bad people; they are simply misguided, inconsiderate, insensitive, selfish, and often times, weak and insecure. Some of them believe that the people they are manipulating are not as valuable as themselves, and that their desires and needs are not as important. This mistaken belief is what allows them to continue to act the way they do without considering the feelings of other people.

Different types of Negative Manipulation:

- **Turning your Emotions against you:** Techniques for manipulation vary widely, but usually, negative manipulators will attempt to get the feelings of others to work against them. They will try to do that by doing or saying things that are intended to stir up fear, anger, shame, guilt, or any other uncomfortable feeling. For example, they might insinuate that if we don't follow through on their suggestions or orders, something horrible will result.

- **Threats of Future Unpleasantness:** They might also try to describe to you all of the different types of unpleasant situations that could arise if you don't do what they want. They might imply or even overtly insist that something is our fault, responsibility, or duty, using ethics and morality to pressure us to come around to their ideas or demands. Some people will even throw every trick at us, warning us of the consequences of disappointing or letting them down.

- **Common Phrases Used:** They may imply to us that we will be so happy if we do what they want us to do, or that we will make them very happy, and that they will love us so much. They may also use phrases like "You need to…" or "You must…" or "You should…" as a way to subtly pressure you into following through on what they are asking of you. They will say those phrases and others which insinuate great consequences if you don't follow the obligation they are giving to you.

What do each of the above methods and techniques share in common with each other? The person doing the negative manipulation doesn't offer anything of value in return for fulfilling their wishes. Instead, the victim gets exploited by a created power imbalance.

How to Avoid being Negatively Manipulated by Others:

So, now that we have discussed some of the signs of negative manipulation, it's time to figure out how to avoid it and recognize when someone is trying to use it on you.

- **Be Aware of your Rights:** The absolute most important rule you can follow when dealing with someone who wants to manipulate you in negative ways is to know your own worth and rights. This way, you will always know when someone is attempting to violate them. So long as others are not getting harmed in the process, you should be defending yourself. Every human should have the right to have differing opinions from others, to protect yourself, to say "no" when you need to, and to decide what's important to you. You should also have the right of expressing your wants, opinions, and feelings, and always be treated with respect.

    Unfortunately, the world has plenty of people who won't want to acknowledge or respect your rights, especially negative manipulators. You will also come into contact with others who generally wish to take advantage at any opportunity. However, you can proudly defy this by letting them know that you are the one who runs your life, no one else.

- **Maintain Healthy Distance:** Another way to tell who is manipulative is to pay attention to the way someone acts in varying situations and in front of various individuals. Although everyone, to a degree, puts on different faces depending on where they are, most people who are harmfully manipulative are extreme about it. They might, for example, be extremely polite and friendly to one person, and completely disrespect another, or act like a victim one second, and then act controlling immediately after.

    If you notice someone acting this way regularly, it's a good sign to distance yourself from them and not engage with them unless it's an absolute necessity. Usually, the reasons behind these types of behavior are complicated, and it isn't your duty or responsibility to help or change that person. Trying to do so will often only lead to suffering on your part, so it's better not to expect much when you notice these signs.

- **Don't Blame yourself:** A person who wishes to manipulate others in harmful ways searches for weaknesses to exploit, so it makes sense that someone who has been victimized by one might blame themselves or feel inadequate. But in a situation like this, you should remember that it isn't you that's the issue here; you are being pressured to feel bad by someone else who is very good at making people feel bad.

    This is how they get their way. Instead, think about the relationship you have with this person and ask yourself if they are respecting you, demanding reasonable things of you, and whether you are both benefiting, or only one of you is. Ask yourself, also, if you feel good about yourself after spending time with this person, or if you would feel better being around them less. The way you answer these questions will lead to important answers about where the issue lies in the situation.

- **Questioning them:** Eventually, this type of person is going to demand or request things from you. Many times, these requests or others will take their needs into consideration, while completely ignoring yours. Next time you receive a solicitation that is completely unreasonable, turn the focus back to them by asking some questions. Ask them if their request is reasonable, or if what they are asking from you is fair. You can also try asking if you get to have an opinion in this matter, or ask what benefit you will be gaining from the arrangement.

    Each time you ask questions like this, you are holding a mirror up to them, allowing them to see what they are truly asking of you. If they are self-aware, they will likely retract their request or demand. But there may be some cases, such as dealing with a narcissist, who will keep insisting without even considering your questions. If that happens, follow these guidelines.

- **Don't Answer Immediately:** One way to combat manipulation is to use time as a resource. Often, the manipulator will not only ask you to fulfill an unreasonable demand, but they will want an answer immediately. When this happens, rather than answering right away, use time and distance yourself from their request and influence. This can be done by telling them that you will think about it. Although these words are simple, they give your power back to you, giving you the option to weigh the advantages and disadvantages of the situation and let you work out something better, if need be.

- **Teach yourself to say "No" when needed:** Saying "no" is difficult for many people, since we are often taught and conditioned to be polite whenever possible. Being able to confidently but politely say "no" comes with learning communication skills. When this is articulated effectively, you can hold onto your self-respect, and also continue a healthy relationship. Keep in mind that your personal rights include deciding what matters to you, being able to turn down a request free from guilt, and choosing health and happiness for yourself. You are responsible for your life, not the person who is making unreasonable demands of you.

- **Create a Consequence:** Next time a negative manipulator tries to violate your rights, and refuses to accept your answer, set a consequence for their behavior. Knowing how to assert and identify appropriate consequences is a crucial skill for standing down someone who is being very difficult or disrespectful. If you can articulate this clearly and thoroughly, your consequences will cause them to pause and stop violating you, shifting to a position of respect.

How to Confront a Bully in a Safe Way:

Not all manipulators resort to bullying, but many of them do. Someone is being a bully when they use intimidation or harm to get what they want from you. Remember, always, that a bully chooses people they see as weak to pick on, and compliance and passivity will only strengthen this. However, a lot of bullies are afraid and insecure deep down, so when their victim starts to stand up for themselves, this will often lead the bully to back off. Whether this situation is occurring in a playground or at the office, it applies, most of the time. Keep in mind that many bullies have actually withstood bullying and violence. Although this doesn't excuse their behaviors, it does help the victim to understand.

Chapter 6: A Guide to Positive Manipulation (Persuasion)

Leadership and manipulation go together, but there is a distinct difference between the type of manipulation discussed in the last chapter, and ethical (or positive) manipulation. Positive manipulation relies on using personal influence to gain a response or outcome. To put it another way, it relies on convincing someone to do what you are asking. This definition makes it easy to understand why the most powerful leaders in the world are often very skilled at ethical manipulation. Regardless of its negative connotations, manipulation is not always a bad thing. Actually, countless leaders in business could enjoy advantages from using some of these methods in their set of skills. One of these skills is using manipulation in a responsible, ethical, and positive way.

What makes Positive Manipulation Ethical?

Positive, ethical manipulation methods have outcomes and goals that have been thoroughly defined, and are always motivated by goal-seeking and accomplishment. It's not appropriate at all to try to manipulate people for pleasure or your own personal achievement, while disregarding their rights or desires. But it is necessary and appropriate to use this tactic as a way to help people achieve shared visions and to further an organization or business.

What to use Positive Manipulation Methods for:

Influence and persuasion skills are extremely useful and powerful for many different reasons. They can be used to convince a child to follow through on something, to change ideas in a county or community, or to help change the minds or actions of employees and customers at work. When you decide to develop these skills and methods, you instantly increase your own personal influence, leadership abilities, and power.

- **Influence:** Ethical manipulation mainly relies on persuading or influencing others to follow through on something they wouldn't do on their own. This could be thoughts or actions, and although the person might naturally choose something else, a leader who ethically manipulates them exerts subtle and appropriate pressure in order to help that person reach an outcome that is most desired.

- **Persuasion:** Subordinates and leaders often disagree on objectives, processes, and concepts, and this is entirely natural. But using techniques that rely on positive and ethical manipulation can help persuade peers or subordinates to come over to the way you think of things. Instead, of overtly pressuring, bullying, or bulldozing, these methods allow you to share your ideas and give them a chance to agree with you or shift to your perspective.

- **Inspiration:** When someone uses manipulation and has the correct motivation behind it, it can actually be very inspiring to the people involved. If, for example, you're looking at a difficult, long project, you can give the team some easy simple projects now in order to help them feel more capable and confident. This is, technically, manipulation, but it's for a good cause and helps the people involved. Manipulation is all about getting people to feel or act in certain ways. For example, getting people to be enthusiastic and exciting about something they are doing.

- **Unity:** Conflicts at work and home are a natural part of social interaction. But it's perfectly possible to manipulate a situation in order to bring about more unity. This relies on recognizing that a conflict is about to happen and finding ways to manipulate the situation to prevent problems. This is a great example of manipulation being a positive, rather than negative, influence. People who can do this are often seen as valuable assets to group situations or work environments, because they know how to mediate and keep the peace. These are valuable abilities to have.

- **For Defending yourself:** There are many benefits to learning about persuasion. Not only is it useful for using it yourself to get things done, but you can use it to protect yourself from manipulation that isn't good for you. For example, perhaps a friend is pressuring you to go out and drink all night when you have to be to work the next morning, just because they don't have to work. Being aware of persuasion tactics will help you to recognize theirs and persuade them to drop the subject. You can also use these tactics to exert your own will and rights in difficult situations.

You can study your surroundings and the people around you in order to find the correct methods for getting done what you need to do. This can be at work, at home, or in your personal friendships and romantic relationships.

Why Compliance Manipulation is Ineffective:

In this section of the book, we're going to consider some main techniques for persuasion that can be used in nearly any situation. But before getting into these methods, we should go over what persuasion means to have a fuller understanding of it. This is crucial to be aware of, since persuasion can often be confused with pressuring others into compliance. The latter is often focused only on changing the behaviors of other people, while persuasion tactics try to get people or groups or people to feel and think positively about the thoughts or actions you wish for them to have.

- **Manipulation for Compliance:** There are lots of ways to manipulate people into complying with your ideas. Some examples of this include threats of legal action if you don't follow laws (like a ticket for not wearing your seatbelt), or a parent threatening their child with punishment for not finishing their homework or cleaning up their room. These are distinctly different from typical techniques for persuasion, because a change of feelings or beliefs is not necessary for the people to act or change their behaviors. They only have to be able to feel the fear and recognize it to comply.

- **Resentment and a Lack of Motivation:** The problem with techniques like the ones listed above is that without the fear or threat, people wouldn't follow through on what they're being asked to do. In addition to this, nobody enjoys being negatively manipulated, meaning that they are more likely to feel resentful of these tactics once they realize what is happening to them. Sadly, this form of manipulation is still very common, but although it can work for some cases, it's not a very sophisticated or effective tool.

When you look back at being manipulated into compliance, either by authority figures at school, bosses at work, or your own parents in childhood, it usually isn't a very good feeling. More often than not, it leads to negative feelings and interactions, and this is because it's based on fear, instead of free will and choice. The question then becomes, how is it possible to get people to do what you want them to do of their own volition? They must make the choice themselves if they are going to continue to choose it.

Using NLP and Creating Agreement for Successful Positive Manipulation:

The trick here is to use agreement to be successful at positive manipulation and persuasion. You have to create a few different levels of agreement, such as spiritual, emotional, mental, and physical. Consider an individual getting carried on by a strong current of water, such as a river. You have to construct a strong enough agreement stream that it pulls the person in your direction. How is this possible to do?

- **Connect:** Studies done in hypnosis and NLP show that establishing rapport with someone else makes them much more agreeable to your ideas, suggestions, and actions. This can be done by subtly mirroring them, as mentioned earlier in the book. Don't think of it as imitating or mocking, but rather as complementing the other person's facial expressions and gestures. This gives them more positive feelings towards you and makes them more suggestible to your ideas.

    If you practice this often and truly understanding the concepts behind establishing connection and rapport with others, you can utilize mirroring and matching as a technique to bring others into positive alignment with yourself. Furthermore, this can be done in such a way that the other individual has no idea that you're using a technique at all. That's because this is a subliminal method that everyone responds to in spite of themselves. This leads to a nice, warm, harmonious sense that the two of you are relating to each other.

- **Trust:** Not many people are aware of the way that nonverbal communication happens between two people, even though this is where the majority of signals are being sent. When you mirror and match someone else's mannerisms and expressions, their subconscious is receiving a message that it's okay to trust you and let their guard down. This is because you are acting like them, and most humans relate easier to people that they see as similar to them. Even if the person doesn't know why on a conscious level, they will feel more comfortable with you.
  Trust is necessary for getting someone to come around to your ideas or goals. It's true that you can pressure someone into going along with what you want, but if there is any chance that they will enjoy it and do it willingly, you have to create rapport and positive feelings in your interactions. Only then is persuasion or ethical manipulation possible.

- **Breaking Patterns:** In addition to mirroring to build rapport, other NLP techniques exist for strong subliminal influence. One example of this is using questions in order to re-direct someone's attention or focus to something else, or to break mental patterns. Questions are effective because they are hard to resist answering. Our minds automatically want to try to solve questions as soon as they are asked. For example, if someone asks you what good things have happened in your life lately, your state of mind automatically begins focusing on positivity.

- **Storytelling and Metaphors:** Another method for persuading others is using storytelling and metaphors to get your point or idea across to them. People who specialize in persuasion can make this tactic very complicated, but it's actually effective right away, in a lot of cases. This can be done by sharing a story that shows you reaching a conclusion that you are hoping they will also reach, using positive descriptive terms. Make sure you are making something sound highly positive, if you want someone to agree with you.

- **Set a Goal:** If you have any desires to accomplish something specific, you have to get specific about defining it. It's too easy to meander through interactions and daily life without having a clear cut vision of what you wish to do. In order to effectively persuade and ethically manipulate others, set a desired goal for the interaction you have with them. This could be to simply call or text them, send a letter in the mail, set up a meeting, or convince them to sign up for something. Decide ahead of time what the action or outcome will be that you wish for the individual to come around to.

- **Get Confident and Passionate:** Become enthusiastic about your service, product, idea, or concept. Enthusiasm is contagious and effective for persuasion. Think about it, when you're talking to someone who is trying to convince you about something, is it easier to listen to them when they are droning on and seem bored out of their minds, or when they seem completely sold on and excited about the idea? It's important to get excited. This can be done by emotionally connecting with whatever advantages and benefits you are providing with your idea. Think about who the idea has helped and will help.

In addition to this, giving logical perspectives is also helpful when it comes to ethical manipulation and persuading people. Keep in mind that people often make their choices based on emotion, and later justify those choices using logical reasons. Appealing to both of these is your best bet.

- **Be Upfront and Ask Directly:** Another technique is to simply ask directly for whatever it is that you want. This might mean a date, asking someone to buy your product, or convincing them to sign up for something. If you don't ask, you will never know! A lot of times, people simply don't know what to do, and offering an action, idea, or solution can be helpful for everyone involved.

Practice all of the skills listed above to help your influence and persuasion skills develop and grow into strong abilities. Becoming great with persuasion and ethical manipulation relies first on understanding the foundations of persuasion, and then using techniques to support them. Keep in mind that as long as you are offering something of value in return for what you are asking of someone, you are using persuasion and influence in a positive way. Being aware of what persuasion and manipulation tactics look like can also help protect you against people trying to use them adversely against you.

Conclusion

Thank you again for purchasing this book!

I hope this book was able to help you to understand how prevalent and important the subject of manipulation is in our everyday lives. Although the word "manipulation" typically has a negative connotation, it isn't always that way. We encounter this phenomenon far more often than we consciously realize, and living the most advantageous life possible means getting in touch with this and using it to your benefit.

With the information in this book, you will never again be taken advantage of by manipulative people without your best interests at heart. In addition to this, you can utilize methods of positive and ethical manipulation to influence and lead others in beneficial ways. When you understand this tool of social power and influence, you can achieve whatever it is you wish to achieve in life. Our worlds are increasingly connected and social, so this is an invaluable skill to develop. Luckily, it can be learned and constantly improved, like any other skill in life

Finally, if you enjoyed this book, then I'd like to ask you for a favor, would you be kind enough to leave a review for this book on Amazon? It'd be greatly appreciated!

Thank you!

Book #4
Manipulation Mastery

How to Master Manipulation, Mind Control, and NLP

Introduction

Congratulations on purchasing this book and thank you for doing so. ***Manipulation Mastery: How to Master Manipulation, Mind Control, and NLP*** is not a beginner's book, but rather a book for those familiar with NLP, mind control, and manipulation techniques.

To learn the basics of these techniques, please refer to the first book in this series, ***Manipulation: The Definitive Guide to Understanding Manipulation, Mind Control, and NLP***, which can be easily found online where you discovered the current title you are reading now. The first book in this series is full of beginner's level information regarding understanding manipulation, and how to learn and apply these applications to get you started!

Within the pages of this book, you will learn effective tactics that every master manipulator employs to exert their influence and control on others. By knowing advanced techniques, tricks, and tools manipulators use to get what they want, you will be able to spot a manipulative person with ease. Manipulative people can be your co-worker, your friend, someone you just met, or someone you even share a bed with. Learning how master manipulators think, what skills they use, and how to spot them will allow you to protect yourself in the event that you find yourself engaged in a relationship with a master manipulator, or how to avoid being manipulated completely!

There are many books on this subject on the market today, purchasing this one was a smart move! Thank you again for your purchase. Every effort was made to ensure this book is as full of useful and practical techniques as possible. Please sit back, and enjoy!

Chapter 1: Avoiding Manipulative Relationships

In the first book of this series, you were introduced to the basics of influence, mind control, NLP, and manipulation. This book delves deeper, into the subtler manipulation tactics that are often used to influence and sway others. A very important aspect to consider when learning how these tactics work, is *learning how to avoid being a victim or target of a manipulator.*

Many master manipulators have psychopathic tendencies, but not all are in fact true psychopaths, or sociopaths. Some people do not even realize they are trying to exert their will onto another against that person's wishes, but there are those that have the express intent of manipulating others. Psychopaths will actually go out and hunt for people to manipulate, but again, not every manipulative person has a mental defect, nor does every manipulator acknowledge or understand what they are doing.

Being able to determine when someone is attempting to sway you or someone close to you is a fine art. By learning to master the arts of manipulation, influence, mind control, and NLP, you are also mastering the art of spotting these tactics sooner, and saving yourself from undue influence.

The techniques discussed in this book cover an array of relationships, from strangers and new acquaintances, to people that you may already be close to. The most difficult aspect of these tactics to digest is when they are employed against another person in an intimate relationship. The psychological damage that these techniques may cause in a significant other or spouse who has been the victimized or targeted by a manipulative person can last for years. Many people manipulated and used in intimate relationships need to seek out professional psychological effect to help them move past this type of emotional and psychological abuse. And make no mistake, these techniques, when employed against a love one, are abuse.

So, how do you stop yourself from becoming involved with a master manipulator before the relationship develops too far? Well, to begin, it depends if you are engaging in a relationship with someone who just has manipulative tendencies but means you no harm, or a master manipulator who expressly wants to control or manipulate you.

Most intentional manipulators have a few characteristics or traits in common. A lack of empathy is often an ear-mark for a manipulator. They are narcissistic or self-absorbed, and they truly are indifferent to others who suffer for any reason. Their indifference may extend to everyone, but you, and that may make anyone feel special. But special or not, beware, because you will eventually be just another person they feel indifference towards. If you experience a small setback that upsets you, a loss, or an illness, take note of your new partner's actions. Do they state that they care verbally, but refuse to engage with you in person or excuse themselves from you to avoid you during your time of duress? If there is any indication that they may not care as much as they say they do, pay attention for other signs.

While we are on the subject of their words and actions, another easy way to separate the manipulators is not by what they say, but in what they do. Master manipulators are known for being charismatic and saying all the right words at exactly the right times, but rarely do their words and actions match one another. Look for unfulfilled promises, saying one thing and then doing another, and opinions that flipflop, depending on who else is around to hear what they are saying. Manipulators may seem to be all-encompassing to their partners, but in public they may tend to fade into the background in order to observe others, or completely change their stances, opinions, or ideas to fit others they are engaged with. Watch for inconsistencies.

Manipulators who intend to cause harm will tell you they adore you, but find small ways to shoot digs at you that may hurt your feelings. If you are dating or in a relationship with someone who states that they want to spend every waking minute of their free time with you, then calls you "needy" or "codependent" when you express a desire to spend time with you, it is sending mixed signals that you may try to excuse away. There could be a million different reasons why neither of you can spend every day together, but there is never a good excuse to indicate that you are the one with issues, especially when they are the ones who initiated the response from you.

Another consideration to mention again is the right and wrong in a disagreement, and what the manipulator will say and do during an argument. Manipulators will fight dirty, insult you, try and use information you have given them against you, and will never admit wrongdoing. At times, master manipulators will deny words or actions they are aware they have done, hoping that this confusion will make you question your view or beliefs on events that have occurred.

They may continue to speak about things that you have expressly stated you no longer want to discuss, creating unease in you, and disregard your discomfort.

Master manipulators will disregard the emotions you express to them. They may refuse to validate the way you feel, or express to you that the way you feel is not accurate or correct. Some manipulative people will begin to completely refuse to acknowledge the feelings of their significant others as the relationship progresses,

Despite all of these negative aspects of the manipulators persona, many people will find that even though they know the relationship is unhealthy, they will continue to engage in the relationship or have an extremely hard time cutting loose from the manipulator. The soaring emotions that excited you in the beginning of the relationship will make you all the more likely to fear losing those strong emotions, and therefore fear losing the manipulator themselves. You may find yourself increasingly unsatisfied in the relationship, and loved ones may notice a change in your mood too, but despite your unhappiness you may find yourself dreading a life without them. Your own mood will begin to be directly controlled by the mood of the manipulator, and you may find yourself attempting to find favor with this person, even though you have done nothing untoward or wrong. Because of the conflicting and confusing aspects of the relationship, you may find yourself overanalyzing or obsessively trying to put your finger on what is really going on. You may notice an increased state or level of anxiety in yourself, as you are unsure of what is happening or where you stand with the manipulative partner. Apologizing or compromising who you are regularly, whether you understand why you feel the need, feeling insecure about yourself in general, or experiencing feelings of guilt or inadequacy are often strong indicators that you are in a relationship with a manipulator.

The best way to protect yourself from engaging in a manipulative relationship is to be aware of their often-subtle manipulation tactics. The next chapter will begin to educate you in the often-used subtle arts of master manipulators, and will include examples of these techniques. Again, it should go without saying that these nuanced tactics can be used by you, or against you, in any interaction, and at any level of familiarity.

Chapter 2: Mastering Subtle Manipulation Tactics

There aren't many individuals who are skilled in the art of manipulation, but with time, effort, and practice, anyone can become one who gets what they want by any means at your disposal. Manipulators sarply focused on following their own interests with less regard to how their pursuits may affects others is necessary for the manipulator. The manipulator must have a great command and understanding of the language of persuasion. Becoming more cultured, more verbal, and generally having greater status, or the suggestion of some sense of authority is key. Most masters of manipulation are utterly charming to say the least.

Once you have begun your pursuits to achieve a greater level of manipulation mastery and understanding, you will find that it becomes easier to spot when someone is attempting to establish more power and authority in relationships, in the workplace, and beyond. You will learn how to manipulators present themselves and their desires in such a way that it not only establishes these powerful dynamics, but how they use the structures they have set in place to work to their advantage. Master manipulators to not tend to appear overly critical on any one stance or opinion to any severe degrees, in fact, they will be unable to effectively manipulate others successfully if they do attempt to employ extreme tactics. Manipulators often sit on the fence on many important issues so as not to offend anyone. Again, it adds to their overall appeal and charm.

You will learn that master manipulators will often learn how to use their knowledge to gain alliance with others to get what they want. The perception of wanting something "for the greater good of all" is an effective tactic, but not necessarily the true goal of the manipulator. The ultimate goal is to influence the thoughts and actions of others, and flexing control they eventually gain over others is key. Manipulators have a strong need to be the one who garners the power to control the way information is presented to the other parties they wish to manipulate. Mastery of utilizing logical or rational thinking to shape other's perception of the appearance of the information they are providing, while maintaining an "objective stance" pseudo-position is key. As manipulators begin to inform others, manipulating how others see the topic comes down to the manipulator keeping from them what you may not want others to consider to win their favor, or by not allowing conflicting information that may harm their stance or allow for other opposing opinions to be heard fairly.

Using Yes As The Only Answer

Manipulating people immediately is a fine art. What do they want from other people? What do they want from you? Manipulators will often work to find ways to form a quick but favorable impressions as fast as possible. A simple, effective way they achieve a fast yet effective connection is to refer to their targets as they want them to be and how they want to be perceived. Here is an example for the individual you meet that you may want to align to your will in the future:

After initial introduction, manipulators will begin to ask questions to garner as much information about the other person and the way they think as possible. All these details may seem basic at first, but it lays the groundwork for comradery, when it suits the manipulator. If they want this individual to agree with them right away, and they don't have a lot of time to lay a solid groundwork for a friendly relationship, they will ask questions of their targets that they know can only be answered with a yes from them. As they ask these yes questions, they will nod, and use body language to their advantage by either mimicking their targets body language or leaning in to create a false sense of agreement. Upon asking an appropriate amount of yes questions, and this will depend upon the topics they are going over and where the manipulator needs the direction of the conversation to go, they will then ask THEIR yes question. Before they even receive an answer, they may subtly nod in anticipation, as if they already agree completely with the yes they are about to illicit from their target.

Using Familiarity

Another effective tactic for unfamiliar personal manipulation is to chat the individual up as they would, again, to garner information they can use to their advantage, and then refer to the individual they are trying to manipulate as they want the pseudo-relationship to be seen by the person they wish to manipulate. Below is an example of how a manipulator may wish to use someone they just met, for the sake of example we will name the target "Bob".

You meet someone at a party named Bob, and upon introduction learn that Bob has acquired great personal wealth, or has an influential or impressive job that may help you attain a goal in the future. After brief introduction, small talk, and pleasantries, introduce the individual as "My new friend Bob." You barely know Bob, but you have just referred to him as you want him to be, your new "friend", and Bob will feel a boost to his ego in your acknowledgement of his importance. Bob will feel that he has impressed you, someone he barely knows, to the point that you already like him enough that you want to be his friend. This subtle boost to his ego will only positively garner his favor. And, by starting off by using flattery is the first step in convincing Bob that he has the upper hand, he is the person others like quickly, and you make him feel good about himself. If you make Bob feel good, Bob will invariably want to befriend you in turn, and will be susceptible to trying to reciprocate these good feelings by being agreeable with you and what you want. And as we know, manipulation isn't really about Bob, it is about what you want from Bob.

As you can see, poor Bob was manipulated almost upon introduction, and probably won't see anything coming. Most people do not anticipate new acquaintances will have ulterior motives immediately, but that is a common mistake. Manipulators are always looking for their newest target.

Observation

The most important tactic you can do to master the art of manipulation and to protect against it yourself is to observe other people in varying degrees. Observation is the single best way to educate yourself in regards to the behavior patterns of other individuals. It does not matter if you are in a close and familiar setting, taking time to sit back and observe your loved ones or close friends, or if you are in a public park, sitting back on a bench and just taking note of strangers and their interactions with one another. By taking a step back to notice others, you are gaining insight into how people communicate with one another, and what small cues their overall behavior patterns mean in day-to-day life. By observing everyone whenever you can, you will soon begin to notice behavior pattern similarities in people who really have nothing in common.

Observing people and their nonverbal or physical language, their miniscule facial expressions, and trying to get a feel for the overall picture that people paint when they communicate with one another will help you recognize a pattern and give you much needed insight into their mindset. As you take note of these cues and small tells while observing people in different settings, you will eventually be able to pick up how another person is thinking and feeling on an almost intuitive or subconscious level. Observing and taking note of small tendencies will become second nature to you over time, and you will be able to take what you notice and use it to your advantage, and also be adept in protecting yourself again from those who wish to manipulate you.

Another positive benefit of using observation to your advantage is that it will aid you in understanding and grasping the concepts of psychology better. How better to know another human, then to have an intimate insight into why people do the things they do, and think the way they think? Improving upon your psychological skills will aid you in not only gaining this insight, but will allow you to better detect lies, be able to discern when someone really does agree with you or is merely trying to placate you, as well as any other myriad of communicable interactions.

Reciprocate To Take

Another tried and true tactic of anyone wishing to master manipulation is to know the value of give and take, or reciprocity. Giving to another, sometimes repeatedly, before asking for anything in return is an almost guaranteed win for you. Offering a shoulder to cry on, loaning out a few bucks without being asked, a listening ear, or just doing something nice for another are small endeavors that reap huge rewards. Often, using generosity can even mask intentions for manipulation at a later date. As an example, let's go back to our new friend "Bob".

We have known Bob for just a few weeks, and already friendship has blossomed into trust, and the manipulator and Bob have almost achieved a confidant status. The reason Bob is so trusting of this manipulator is because they have asked questions, and continued to show genuine interest in Bob and his life. The manipulator has also been observing Bob and the way he interacts in different settings around different groups of people.

Bob works hard and makes good money, and the manipulator wants Bob to invest some of that hard-earned cash into their pockets so they can open a new business. And, while Bob is a respected businessman himself with plenty of money, maybe Bob doesn't have the best luck when it comes to his home life. So, being the great friend they are, the manipulator will go out of their way to make themselves available to Bob. If Bob wants to complain about his spouse, they are there for him to lament to, and the manipulator always see his side. When Bob forgets to call the lawn care service and his grass is tall and his spouse complains, they will show up unannounced and mow it themselves for Bob if need be. They will pick up the tab when going out to lunch, offer a ride, anything they can do for Bob without coming off as creepy or obsessed. So, when they manipulator has finally determine that they have met the reciprocity quotient, they will then ask Bob for that loan.

Bob may not want to loan that much money to anyone, and he may even say no, but by asking for more than they wanted to begin with, they manipulator has already set up the conditions for Bob to feel obliged to say yes to something. After all, look at how much they have done for Bob, and what a good friend they are, right? So, if Bob does in fact say no to the initial amount, he will have been manipulated enough by then that he will more than likely say yes to the smaller amount the manipulator will then suggest further into the conversation. And that amount is what the goal was all along for the manipulator. See how that works?

Use Trust To Gain Trust

Trust is one aspect that cannot be overlooked when considering manipulation. People that do not feel you are genuine will never trust another. A great way to get individuals to trust you, is to trust them first. By giving information, or laying knowledge about yourself or something that involves or effects your life in some way at the feet of another person, you are entrusting them. By showing trust, you are allowing the other individual to feel that you are vulnerable, that they have power in the relationship because you trust them, and they in turn will be more comfortable in reciprocating trust. Entrusting others is tricky, and what you entrust them with is important as so not to diminish their view of you in any way. Another aspect to consider when employing this manipulation technique is to be very careful to not give too much to the other party, lest they be able to use what you have entrusted them with against you later. Again, this is a tactic used by manipulators regularly, so when someone entrusts information to you, take a step back and consider if the information they are giving you really is important to their overall image, or if it is less intimate of the information they want you to entrust in them in turn. If someone is giving the impression of trust, but asking more from you than they are willing to put into you, then they may be trying to appear to trust you, while all the while their true intentions may not be trusting you at all, and more about how much they can convince you to trust them so they may be able to use that trust against you later.

Making Fallacies Do The Work

A fallacy is a mistaken belief, or an ideal that is based on an unsound argument. Fallacies can be easily used in the art of persuasion and manipulation, and there are many to choose from when considering manipulators and their goals, whatever they may be. When manipulators wish to persuade another person, sometimes the best defense is a strong offense. One way they may attempt to distract someone they see as an opponent, or someone they wish to confuse in order to more easily manipulate the conversation is to bombard them with questions to catch them off guard. When communicating with someone they know will not be easy to persuade, manipulators will often begin by immediately asking multiple questions in one sentence. The questions themselves do not need to be related, let alone relevant to the issue at hand, the only important aspect is that there are many of them. Below is an example of how a manipulative person may use fallacies to their advantage to influence another. Take note to recall this technique, lest you be the victim in this tactic:

Say you are heading into a meeting, and you see a co-worker you know will be against or not easily swayed to your idea. Approach them just before or during the beginning of the meeting and ask run on questions. An example would be:

"Hi Joan how have you been, did you see the latest numbers they look great if we stay on the right track per my model, and by the way did I see you and your husband at the bar on the corner last night, how is your husband by the way?"

Joan doesn't know where to start. Should she say she is doing well, let you know her husband is well, deny that it was them you saw last night at the bar, or tell you she thinks your model is full of holes? Joan has just been completely confused and befuddled, and she is more likely to reflect on the personal questions asked of her, which may make her forget to speak up during the meeting about what her concerns are regarding the model.

Repetition is another fallacy that works like a charm when wishing to persuade and manipulate someone else's ideas or thoughts on a subject. Repeat something enough, and it becomes true. Repeat it to enough people enough times, and it may as well be carved in stone. Using ridicule in persuasion is effective as well, as nobody wants to be seen as foolish or to be made fun of. When you ridicule another person, their opinions or ideas, you are in essence placing the thing you are ridiculing in a lower position than yourself and your own opinion or idea. Humor and wit go along well when choosing to ridicule an opposing view, as it takes the sting out of the negative words to observers (hey, they get a little chuckle out of it even), but it seems to drive the ridicule home to the person on the receiving end even more so. When using ridicule, manipulators are careful not to be too mean, less it negatively impact their public persona or image. You will find that people who are ridiculed or have beliefs that are ridiculed tend to be avoided by others, lest they be associated with the lower status or standard of the label you have placed upon it-them.

Using the "false dilemma" technique to persuade another person is also an effective means by which manipulators reach to attain their goals. The idea is to offer two options or outcomes in an argument, and to discuss outcomes depending upon the two different routes that can be taken. One is a negative outcome, the other outcome being what the manipulator wants to happen, or what choice they want the other party to make. Going over the pros and cons of both choices, and highlighting the choice they want the other person to agree with is a complete distraction technique that works very well. Who said there are only ever two choices or options to any dilemma in life? Usually there are many more scenarios and possible outcomes involved, but by focusing the other party's attention to the "this or that" dilemma, a manipulator knows that this takes the targets mind completely away from that basic fact, and they are more likely to be persuades, influenced, or swayed. Another fallacy that is effective in manipulating the answer hoped for is the "false compromise". Most extreme viewpoints are not necessarily correct, let alone accepted by most people, simply because they are extreme in nature. Many people are averse to risk and confrontation, and using the desire others have to not rock the boat to a manipulator's advantage is always a good tactic. The focus on one extreme or another is a great way to get the focus from what is necessarily the better or right answer, and focuses more on compromising viewpoints that work for "everyone as a whole", or "the greater good". The middle of the road is not always the right path to take, but at least it appears to be more inclusive and appealing than an extremist viewpoint.

There are literally hundreds of fallacious argument and debate tactics that are at the manipulators disposal, just waiting on them to pluck them from the air to manipulate another person's ideas, make a clear case everyone can agree on, or to persuade others to agree with them.

An important thing to remember is that most skilled manipulators will never get what they want and run. If they have successfully gotten an individual to agree with them by using persuasion tactics, or have manipulated the minds of a room full of people, manipulators will never simply walk away as soon as they have achieved their goal. It is always vital for the master manipulator to allow for a little banter and chit-chat, and end the conversation on a lighthearted or good note. People tend to recollect the beginning and ending of a conversation. And, they never want to make the other party feel dumped once they have gotten what you want. Any friend or acquaintance persuaded or manipulate today, can easily become an enemy later. Master manipulators will always make an effort to make people happy or comfortable with their interactions with them at the start and end, even if the middle is rocky. The middle is where they have gotten what they wanted, but by leaving others feeling decent about the interaction will tend to make targets even more pliable in the future.

False Victimization

Nobody ever really wants to be a victim, and who in their right mind would want other people to see them as a victim? People feel bad for victims, and most would do anything to make a victim of some wrong feel better, no? When considering manipulation on a subtle level, playing victim can benefit manipulators much more than it can hurt them. Manipulators in the scenario can effectively gain sympathy and compassion from others simply by playing the victim. Most individuals hate to see another person suffering, especially if that suffering is not of their own creation, and will go out of their way to try and help the "victim" in this case suffer less.

For example, let's say you go out with a group of friends for the evening, and Kate knows she don't have enough money to pick up her tab or catch a cab afterwards. Towards the end of the evening, Kate begins to let loose and "confide" about how she has been victimized to garner empathy, and more than likely manipulate someone else into picking up the bill or paying the cab fare for her. This manipulation tactic will look something like this:

"I have been working so hard to make everyone happy at work, I even finished my project early! Then, today, I find out my partner had somehow taken all the credit and everyone was looking at me like I was a lazy coattail rider. I can't afford to lose my job because my partner is a scumbag and chose to lie about who did what. I can't even really afford a cab ride home! I don't know what to do!"

You and your friends will feel bad for Kate, and empathize with her regarding the "horrible" co-worker, and most likely pay for the cab and the bill to make Kate feel better. Because that's what good people do, they help victims.

As you can see, there is a myriad of techniques and tactics that can be used to subtly persuade others to get what you want. Learning to take note of how people interact, doing a little research into the psychological mindset of the person or group of people you wish to persuade, and simple exercises in observation will get you far in your endeavors, but more importantly, you will be better able to spot a manipulator a mile away.

Chapter 3: NLP Mastery & Everyday Applications

As you by now know, Neuro-linguistic Programming (or NLP) was founded on the theory and premise that people process everything through neurological means, our language, and programming deigned from life experiences. NLP practitioners believe that since the neurological system regulated overall bodily functions, and that language determines how we communicate with others, the two aspects go together specifically to dictate how we are programmed, or how we behave, and that these programmed behaviors can be altered both within ourselves, but used to persuade other individuals as well.

NLP modeling is the process of reconstructing superiority. We can model all human behaviors by mastering the beliefs, physiology, and the specific thought methods that trigger the ability or behavior. It is about achieving a specific result from another person by learning how that other person goes about their own individual way of thinking. Following NLP models require that manipulators be able to transfer what the "experts" think they know, and shifting that knowledge into everyday applications for a manipulators own designs. Next, we will go over a couple of popular NLP models, and give examples of how to follow them to become aware of NLP tactics that manipulators can use to gain control over others.

The Milton Model

The Milton Model is a useful form of NLP that uses language to induce and maintain hypnotic states. There are three main aspects of the Milton model: rapport, overloading tactics, and finally, indirect interpretation.

In consideration of the first step of building rapport, observation skills need to be honed specifically to better build the bond or relationship that a manipulator desires to achieve. Taking note of eye movements, and the way an individual tilts the head or ears, is an important task manipulators work on to begin building rapport as it indicates to exactly how the person's mind works to store information. If you notice another individual using more eye cues, making statements like "I see", that leads the other person to subconsciously feel as though you are similar. Comments that start with "I hear" geared towards an individual who uses physical cues that indicate they are more auditory allow for the other party to feel "heard" by the manipulator, and again, evoke a feeling of similarity between the manipulator and their mark. By noticing and duplicating the way in which another individual communicates, they are immediately giving the other party signals that both of them are a "we" who see things in the same light. Manipulators will often employ observation and begin to mirror another's way of speaking and physical mannerisms to help them build rapport faster. Without being obvious, manipulators will slowly begin to mirror the other party's physical stance or posture, begin cautious not make fast or immediate changes to their own stance. As initial communication unfolds, manipulators will then begin to also use the same speaking tone and volume as the other person does. Even beginning to match their breathing patterns to the target's own will create a sense of cohesiveness. Another way manipulators build rapport is to find a commonality between themselves and the other person, even if it is miniscule or under false pretense on their part. The goal of the master manipulator is to build a relationship out of thin air, being careful not to commit to any common experience that can be disproved later and break trust. Manipulators will know they have successfully built rapport with another person by then testing them. If the target is speaking slowly, they will begin to do the same, and then slowly begin to increase the pace of their speech pattern. If the individual in question matches the manipulators pace in return, rapport has been established. Another way manipulators will often test to determine if the rapport has been built successfully is by paying close attention to the reactions to what they say that the other person shows. Manipulators are always assessing, and considering questions like: "Are the responses and facial reactions they wanted to illicit in others being conveyed back to them effectively?" If so, the manipulator knows that they are now in.

The second aspect of the Milton model, referred to as overloading is not to say that the manipulator is overloading the person they wish to perform NLP techniques on, but rather that they are overloading the other person's conscious with vague language to help access their subconscious mind. One of the easiest techniques Milton described was to use a subtle conversational hypnotic tactic often referred to as the double bind. The double bind gives the appearance of two choices, answers, or outcomes, but either response gives the manipulator the desired outcome. When people assume they have a choice between one thing or another, they are more likely to cooperate and focus on the two choices before them. The presupposition of only two choices is accepted unconsciously, and very rarely will the person choose outside of the two options given, despite the obvious fact that there is always another choice. Consider when dining out, the waiter will ask "will you be paying with cash or would you like to use your card?" The presupposition is that you are not going to try and break the law, and of course you are paying for your meal. But, what choice in the matter are you really being given? None. You are paying for your meal. It is a perfect example of a double binding question.

Now that presuppositions have been mentioned, it should be understood that these are also very effective modes of altering another's thoughts in an almost imperceivably way. Presuppositions are the things stated that are assumed in conversation, whether they truly are or you wish them to be so. Statements like "So, are you going to attend the party before or after the kids go to sleep?", or "Will you be finishing that up today or tomorrow morning?", are good examples of presupposing statements. Was the individual given a choice to not attend the party at all, or not finishing up whatever task was asked about? No. They were given the option of when they were going to do what you wanted them to do.

There are many other techniques Milton discussed regarding this second step, including asking tag questions, or statements that include a question at the end, using language that is ambiguous in nature to confuse the mind, using utilization to take advantage of your intentions, or using unspecified verbs during a conversation all help a manipulator confuse the conscious mind and allow the other person to be open to subliminal suggestions they want to influence on their targets.

The third facet of Milton's model is to use metaphoric speaking to leave what they are saying open to interpretation by the other party. Whether using a well-known metaphor, or one of their own creation, manipulators make sure that the metaphor is relative to the conversation or issue at hand. This will help the other individual relate the current communication to another instance, and leave them using more of their subconscious brain that they would in normal conversation. Tapping into the subconscious mind in one of the ultimate goals of the master manipulator.

Other NLP Tactics

Sometimes, the best way for a manipulator to get what you want is to ask the right question at the right time. Or even better, why not frame the question in the correct way to get the right, or their desired, response to begin with? A very useful technique for manipulators is to use the subliminal persuasion technique of conversational hypnosis to basically tell the other person what they want the answer to be, then ask the question in such a way that their mark will obviously sway their answer to what they think is the "correct" response. By using this skill, manipulators don't have to literally say out loud what they want to hear from others, because doing so could cause the other person to retaliate or refuse. When this maneuver is done properly, the person the manipulator wishes to persuade thinks they are the one who has come up with the correct response all on their own. And how could anyone deny or refute something they themselves have thought up? A great example of this would be if a manipulator were trying to convince someone way out of their league on a date. The manipulator may start the interaction as follows:

"I know I am probably not your type at all, nor you mine, but isn't the same old so boring? Aren't you ready to try something different too?"

This tactic is very useful, and by throwing in an acknowledgement that they aren't necessarily the archetype of the other person's typical idea of dating material, but also that they aren't their norm either, the manipulator is leveling the playing field to their advantage. The target or mark will have no idea what the manipulators type is, all they know is that they aren't it. Interesting how someone out of your league can quickly begin to wonder what league they themselves are really in, isn't it?

Learning Neuro-Logical Levels

Probably the most helpful tool for a manipulator in the NLP arsenal is learning and understanding the Neuro-Logical Levels model. This model maps people and their distinctive personalities into six different groupings based on three aspects: thinking, feeling, and actions. Utilizing this model allows manipulators to comprehend in a clear and organized method what drives another person. The Neuro-logical levels model can be assessed while actively communicating with another person, and is broken down in the following way by the manipulator:

Identity: What is the other person's self-esteem level? Are they happy with their image, both how they see themselves and how others perceive them? How do you identify with this person? Do you both have families?

Environment: Where are you now, and how is the other person positively or negatively responding to the current surroundings?

Behavior: How is this person acting? What good or positive behavioral tendencies are you noticing? Are there any negative behaviors being exhibited, and if so, why? Facial expressions, posture, nonverbal cues, all need to be taken into consideration.

Skills: What skills does this person have as it relates to the situation or interaction? What skills are they lacking? Are they aware of any skills they are lacking in or anything they excel at?

Beliefs: What are their beliefs and values that they hold dear? Do any of these core belief systems help or hinder this person? Do they align with my own values, or is there a way to align them with mine?

Mission: What is this person's motivation? Where are they trying to get in life? What are their hopes, their contributions, what is the central vision or goal they have for themselves?

By using this model and developing their ability to hone in on these questions and the answers given by their targets, the manipulator is learning how to understand and communicate to their advantage at a much faster pace. This structured way of observing and analyzing another person while they are communicating will further enable the manipulator to interact easily with many different types of individuals successfully, as they can discover what makes other people tick, and then they use it to help them manipulate the interaction.

Chapter 4: Mind Control Maven

Emotions are the source of almost every motivation another person has. Sure, logical thinking, reasoning, and ethics all play a role in determining why a person feels, thinks, or acts as they do, but behind all of the above factors, always lies emotional motivation. Mind control is not necessarily some nefarious scheme, but is an effective technique to persuade or win others over. Emotions can be elicited any number of ways, and if you are the one inducing a specific emotion in another person or group, then you are in control. Keep in mind however, that these tactics can also be used against you, so knowing what to be vigilant of is key.

There are many techniques of mind control to consider, from the practical and easily applicated, to brain-wave music and neuroscience. For the purpose of controlling the mind of another, we will be steering specifically towards mind-control tactics that can be used in varying levels to persuade and manipulate.

Drop Love Bombs

The term love-bombing is sort of crude, but it is an easy explanation of a very effective mind-control technique. To love-bomb another person is to make them feel loved, accepted for who they are regardless of any faults, and to create an emotional bond with the other person that they cannot fathom life without. In a romantic relationship, love-bombing is the follow-up to grooming. Once an individual has been effectively groomed by another who wishes to exert influence and manipulation over someone, their next goal is often to make the targets ideal of romantic interactions their new reality. With societal inundation of romantic comedies, books, and television, people often have a very skewed perception of what real romantic love looks like. The entertainment industry has set an unrealistic standard of what a romantic relationship looks like, and that can be used against anyone who hopes for romance like they see in movies. Good morning texts, calls or emails, followed up by repeated check-in interactions throughout the day, and making plans as often through the week as you can be often where this tactic starts. Flattery will get you everywhere, and manipulators know that. Telling the other person how perfect they are on a regular basis, how unbelievable it is to have found a soul-mate, and referring to the future of the relationship often would have anyone thinking that the partner in question is almost too good to be true…so manipulators often take special care to not overdo

their declarations of love too much in the early stages. Including the other person in their inner circle, inviting them to associate with friends and family also help solidify the idea that you believe they are serious, and that what they say is all true. It is easy to become so bombarded with unyielding declarations of love and appreciation, they never stop to think as to whether or not the other person is in fact being sincere, or if they are being manipulated or swayed in any way. And especially considering romantic relationships, once a manipulator has someone in their grasp, they will do almost anything to ensure that the other person seeks out the continued affections and approval. When considering platonic relationships and this technique, instead of heaping on romantic notions and actions, it is all about understanding, acceptance, and teaming up. By including another in as many social and intimate activities as possible to make them feel like part of an inclusive, if not exclusive or tight-knit circle, manipulators work to create bonds that seem deeper than others they may currently have with friends or family members in their life. This manipulation tactic again feeds the human desire to belong, and is effective in eliciting loyalty from the individual.

Creating Ambiance

If a manipulator controls the environment or surroundings, they can manipulate the tone of another person's attitudes or emotions before any words are even spoken. Creating an environment that will be comfortable to the individual or group of people they wish to influence will be dictated by what it is that the manipulator wishes to precisely gain from the other party. If they want the other party to be relaxed and open, using dimmer lighting, and adjusting the temperature to a slightly cooler setting will encourage the person in question to relax and let their guard down. Seating that is comfortable, or casual, if not appearing close and haphazard will only create a sense of intimacy that will further their ambitions. If the goal is to create an intimidating or focus driven atmosphere, using brighter lighting, harder seating, and raising the temperature in the room will cause the individual (or people) to be forced to pay closer attention to the person who is attempting to influence them as they become hyper aware of their slight discomfort. They will be more likely to want to conclude the conversation sooner, and that is the manipulators opportunity to get things done faster.

Using Stress For Gains

When it comes to stress, this is an effective skill manipulator enjoy employing on others, but it is fair to be reminded that if too much stress or pressure is applied at the wrong time, it can easily backfire. The stress of "peer pressure" or public humiliation is a great tactic, but specific parameters must already be in place so as not to cause withdrawal in the individual. Physical stress, or destress, is also useful to manipulators, but again must be applied with caution. Having an important discussion with someone who you want to persuade or manipulate when they are tired, hungry, or need to use the bathroom is a quicker way to get them to agree with you, but only if the situation dictates that this tactic may work. Manipulators understand this, and know how and when to use basic human needs to their advantage. Other times, these physical needs can easily overshadow the goals a manipulator is trying to attain by taking focus away from what they are saying and drawing it directly to their own needs. Be sure that adding stress or stressful factors into the communication will only benefit the manipulators cause, not detract from their goal.

Guilt

Guilt is a powerful emotion, one that causes immediate emotional reactions in people. Using guilt to your advantage is a good technique manipulators often use to get dependency, or loyalty from another. Whether the guilt imposed upon them stems from a personal failure, a fear or phobia, or something that was done by them that can be perceived as a "wrong" does not matter, only that the emotion is evoked by the manipulator when they need to use guilt to get what they want. Certain people can easily manipulate a situation by expressing hurt feelings towards the person they wish to control by basing the reasons for the discontent based on a "perceived wrong". Whether or not the individual actually did anything to upset them is beside the point, the point is that the manipulator wants them to feel like they have. People that feel guilt or shame are more pliable, agreeable, and to a degree feel they deserve some punishment of sorts for the wrong they have committed. Say your partner needs a new phone charger, but doesn't have the money to pick one up, or simply doesn't want to be bothered with leaving the house to go get one. You then come home from work with a soft drink from a local gas station. A manipulator will guilt to get their partner to go get them what they want!

1: "You stopped by the gas station on your way home and didn't even bother to call and ask if I needed anything. How could you be so inconsiderate?"

2: "I didn't realize it would be that big of a deal, I am sorry."

1: "No, I don't suppose you would bother to think of me or my needs at all!"

2: "I apologize, I really didn't think it would bother you so much. Do you need me to go get you something?"

1: "Well, I could really use a new charger for my phone, unless it's going to be a big deal."

2: "No, it isn't a big deal. I will go pick you up one now."

Stopping by the gas station on the way home from work is not a major crime, and chances are they may not even sell phone chargers. But, accused by your spouse or significant other of not thinking of their needs, has made the other party feel bad for it. So, they were more than willing to leave again, just to make amends for the perceived transgression.

Gaslighting

Gaslighting is a term used to describe a very useful manipulation tactic that makes an individual question their own reality by denying that certain events or conversations took place at all. If the manipulator claims they did not do or say what they are accused of, it calls into question the other person's reality, or at least their own perception of events. By denying and refusing to validate the other person's feelings tied to an event that "did not occur", the other party will inadvertently be forced to question themselves, and eventually begin to wonder if they aren't losing it. Gaslighting works best in manipulation when a base relationship has already been set into place and other persuasion and manipulation tactics have been employed, such as already having a well-established rapport and emotional connection. Examples of gaslighting may include denials such as:

"What are you talking about? I have NEVER said that!"

"You never have been good at recalling what actually happened, it's always about what you want to have happened."

"I don't understand where you got that idea from!"

"Are you seriously calling me a liar?!"

By employing gaslighting techniques, manipulators are not only calling into question the other person's memory, they are also calling into question their character and motives. Despite the fact that the manipulator is the one with the agenda, this is a quick and effective way for them to flip the negative connotations from themselves and back onto the other party. Gaslighting is a tactic that works best if it is repeated over time, with the other person beginning to question their perception of reality over time as the manipulator continues to gaslight them when the opportunity arises.

Chapter 5: Traits of Easily Manipulated People

So, you are well versed in the arts of persuasion, NLP, mind control, and manipulation tactics, and you know what to look for. But the question remains; how does a person with manipulative tendencies determine who is easier to influence and manipulate as opposed to other people? Here are some characteristics and traits commonly found in individuals that are likely prey for manipulators.

Caregivers

People that define their lives or self-worth by their contributions to others are often easy to manipulate. These individuals sense of worth is directly related to how much and how often they do for others.

People in Transition

Whether the transitional phase of the other person's life revolves around a career change, educational advancement, or someone who is simply seeking out different life path options, these individuals are looking to make changes, and that fact itself makes them more vulnerable to manipulation techniques. Another example of someone in transition is someone who has recently relocated and is unfamiliar with their new surroundings.

People Pleasers

While people like to be appreciated and accepted for who they are, there are those that have to make everyone happy all the time to feel worthwhile. The idea that they have displeased or upset someone else creates such a negative feeling within themselves, that they will do almost anything to avoid upsetting you, or anyone else. These individuals are easily swayed by skilled manipulators, as they associate their fears of upsetting anyone directly to their own value.

Yes People

This is a group of people that like people pleasers, want to make others happy with them. They have a hard time saying no, no matter how big or small a request may be. These people have a hard time setting boundaries for themselves, so it will be fairly easy for people with bad intentions to cross any lines with them with minimal effort. The person who possesses this characteristic trait has a very hard time being assertive, and that works out great for the manipulator.

Life Changes

People that are in the process of making or undergoing significant life changes are already feeling ambiguous about everything. Life changes like the birth of a new child, or a new empty-nester that is learning how to live without a houseful of children for the first time, individuals that are entering into new phases of life, like just starting out on their own, or people that are recently retired, all have the same thing in common: They are unsure of what is going to happen next, what the next steps are, and how this new phase they are entering should look. They literally are just waiting around for someone to assert influence over them and take up their reigns on their behalf.

Capitalizing on Loss

This sounds like a negative prospect, and it is, because loss itself is unpleasant, a person experiencing a recent loss can literally be putty in the wrong hands. Loss does not necessarily equate a death, sufferers of loss can include those that are going through a divorce or loss of employment, or the loss of their home or business. These individuals are so focused on what they have lost, they will never see manipulation maneuvers coming, and are unlikely to won't put up any fight at all.

Codependent People

Codependent people rely on other people to meet all their needs. This characteristic is by far one of the easiest to manipulate, as they expect you to make them happy, to meet their needs, and for overall support. This type of individual is literally laying their lives in your hands, and basically expecting you to verify their usefulness to you. Codependent people will actually look to you to validate who they are, and you are able to manipulate them with ease using both easy and more advanced levels of manipulation. These individuals are basically asking you to dictate to them who they should be, how they should think, and what others should expect from them.

Identity Crisis

People experiencing a crisis in their identity have no clue who they are or what their true self includes. They may be experiencing this crisis as a result of a life altering experience, or simply lack a strong sense of self in general. They do not have a firm grasp on what their beliefs should be, and can easily be misled by manipulators in the direction they choose to steer them towards. Their opinions, ideas, and values can all be easily altered by influence. A crisis in identity can be experienced by anyone, even those who formerly had a strong sense of who they are and what their life consisted of. Major life events like divorce, trauma, recent betrayals, and even something as simple as stress can alter an individual's idea on who they are in relation to the world.

Chapter 6: Where To Be On Guard

Anyone can be manipulated by someone well versed in the mastery of manipulation, but where do the easiest people to influence and persuade tend to congregate? Well, that depends upon whether the manipulator has a specific target in mind, or if they are just looking for someone they don't already know to test their manipulation mastery skills out on. Below is a list of places that offer a consistent stream of new people to manipulate, and where to be on your guard. Some of these places may be obvious, while others may surprise you. Remember that a master manipulator has no scruples and will go after anyone they see as easy prey, or even seek out specific people they feel may have wronged them in the past. Be vigilant in the following settings:

Bars, Clubs, or Restaurants

Within the walls of bars and clubs, you will find a steady stream of strangers easily observed in a casual setting. Dining locations that are casual in nature, and allow patrons to sit and loiter at will while making nominal purchases are also good places that allow for covert people watching and the opportunity for manipulators to overhear conversations, and take note of any signs of easily manipulated characteristics in others. A good example would be a local coffee shop or bistro. The public atmosphere also creates a false sense of security within potential targets, as their guard is more likely to be down. Be keen to the charismatic individual you meet by pure "happenstance" at the local café who seem utterly perfect for you!

Schools, Colleges, or Lectures

Any of these locations offer a very interesting dynamic…an imbalance of power or authority. Within the walls of education lay teachers and mentors, and these are people that others look up to. People in attendance are looking for guidance and offering their attention and compliance before they ever walk in the door. Manipulators know how to take advantage of this pre-set mindset to test their abilities out on others.

Support Groups

While it may seem less than desirable to someone who is not intentionally out to manipulate others, people that attend support groups are looking for support and understanding. They are open to a shoulder to cry on, and are already prepared to trust within the confines of the group setting. Attendees are already in vulnerable states, otherwise they wouldn't be there. Pay attention to friendships that are formed in these types of group settings. Not everyone is always there for honest reasons.

Travel Settings

Whether on an airplane, train, or cruise ship, people that are travelling are unfamiliar with their environment and are focused more on calibrating the environment rather than the people they encounter. People are also friendlier during travel, and are even looking for new people to meet and interact with, making them more open to communicating with strangers. It is easy for manipulative people to create a pseudo-alliance or sense of comradery with another person if they think they are both new to the location or experience as well. Vacation is a prime environment for a manipulator to spot out people to influence and manipulate for their own gains, so be mindful of interactions when you are travelling.

Online

Whether you are surfing an online forum or group, or initiating contact with another person via a dating website, the internet places the whole of the world at our fingertips when it comes to meeting people and there are without a doubt people lurking online who are expressly looking for people to manipulate. There are some drawbacks to manipulators that target others online, as they may not be able to actually meet the target in person, but it is a very useful way to test manipulation mettle. Whether they are looking to see if they can get others to agree with them, or trying to talk someone they don't even know into doing their bidding, the internet is a safe place for manipulators to hone their skills. Behind the safety of a screen, manipulators can become anyone, say anything, and use all the skills they have with ease. Social media sites offer millions of potential marks. It is just as easy to set up a fake or false account and email as it is a legitimate one. Obviously, manipulators won't be able to employ certain tactics like some practiced in NLP in regards to the observation techniques, but they will be able to determine just how far their words alone can get them with others. Manipulators often look for lonely people to exploit online.

Alumni or Networking Events

Networking settings offer a commonality component, that means the manipulator will not need to create a false sense of sameness in their efforts to manipulate another, the parameters are already in place. You are both present for a specific purpose, so you already have things in common in the mind of the target of a manipulator. How much easier will it be for them to manipulate another person in this setting, as they already assume you have a like-minded goal? Alumni events offer a similar but different benefit, a common and shared experience (in this case, attending the same school), but may also offer a sense of familiarity within the other party. The past can also create a sense of happier times in many people, and put them at ease and make them less guarded. Alumni and class reunion events are where manipulators hunt, as they are easier to create a false sense of connection. Beware of the charmer you went to school with but never really knew, they may end up being nothing charming about them.

Political, Campaign, or Movement Events

In settings involved with politics, campaigns, or political movements, there is an element of intense emotion. Emotions are every manipulator's best friend, as they are what drives other people and everything they think, say, and do. Also, creating a sense of agreement or alliance makes for a false sense of comradery, of being alike. Sharing powerful emotions or experiences can boost certain hormones in the brain that can signal equally strong emotions of closeness, or even love. Sharing these bonds, whether they are real or not, only adds to the intensity of the interaction and subsequent follow up interactions when meeting people in these surroundings. And all the emotions and variables about work directly in the favor of the manipulator.

Conclusion

As you can see, mastering the art of manipulation takes time and effort, but with practice the benefits can be endless. You will learn how to spot manipulation and influence tactics from the most basic techniques to the most advanced. NLP and mind control techniques are not hard to recognize, once you remember that knowing the skills of a master manipulator will help you protect yourself and others from these controlling and sometimes devastating interactions.

Remember to check out the beginning title in this series, **Manipulation: The Definitive Guide to Understanding Manipulation, Mind Control, and NLP** if you haven't already. The first book is a great starting point to learn the basic workings of these tactics and how they are applied to everyday life.

Thank you for wanting to improve your abilities and knowledge, and for the purchase of this book. We hope that you were adequately provided the additional tools needed to reach your full potential in mastering these fine arts.

Now that you are finished reading and furthering your knowledge, the next step is to practice being on the lookout for what you have learned. You are an individual and can free-think, arm yourself against those that want to manipulate others for their own gain.

Finally, if you found this book useful in anyway, please give this book a positive review on Amazon, it will be much appreciated. Having a positive review from you will help this book reach many more people, so that they can benefit from the information shared within this book as well.

To your success!

Book #5
Manipulation

The Complete Step-by-Step Guide on Manipulation, Mind Control, and NLP

Introduction

Congratulations on purchasing your personal copy of *Manipulation: The Complete Step-by-Step Guide on Manipulation, Mind Control, and NLP.* Thank you for doing so.

The following chapters will discuss some of the many ways you can manipulate the thoughts, beliefs, and behaviors of others and how you can recognize when that same manipulation is happening to you.

You will discover how important our step-by-step guide is to identifying manipulative strategies and techniques that are being used to persuade you to do another's wished, and how quickly you can turn the tables and apply those same steps to achieve your desired outcome.

The final chapter will explore what you consider to be an active and fruitful way to use these steps. You are in control; the decision is yours. Will you use our step-by-step guide to help yourself and others toward a positive outcome? Or, will you choose to practice the darker side of manipulation and mind control?

There are plenty of books on this subject on the market; thanks again for choosing this one! Every effort was made to ensure it is full of as much useful information as possible. Please enjoy!

Chapter 1: Manipulating the Mind through NLP

Before we discuss the positives and negatives of manipulation through NLP, let's define the term, shall we? NLP stands for Neuro-Linguistic Programming. I'm sure that definition holds no meaning for most of you, so we'll explain it a bit further. The three words in the term NLP all represent elements that contribute to how our bodies function, what makes us think as we do, and how we form our perceptions. Ultimately, we think, believe, and behave based on those three things, and those things create our reality. This school of thought promotes the idea that there is no actual reality, only that which an individual creates through his or her NLP. Let's break down the term a bit more.

Neuro

This element oversees our bodily functions and reactions.

Linguistic

This element determines how we communicate with ourselves and others.

Programming

This feature combines our past experiences and relates it to our immediate perceptions to determine our future behaviors, which become our new reality.

The step-by-step guide on manipulation we will be discussing throughout this book is not meant to be used as a negative tool to forcefully control others, although it can. Instead, we offer these five steps to help you identify when you are being manipulated and, ways that you can persuade others to your way of thinking if it is in their best interest. When you have the other person's well-being as your primary motivation, using these five steps will help you lead them to a more positive outcome. However, if your motives are selfish, practicing these measures will only serve to frustrate you and create distrust in those you are trying to persuade.

As you read through these chapters, it may be the first time you've ever thought of manipulation in a positive light, so let's give you some examples of the power of manipulation and how to use it to benefit others and help you get your desires as well.

The Awesome Power of Manipulation

There is a theory out there that most of us experience manipulation every day, and that our freedom of choice has been slowly taken away by societal programming that has gradually changed our perception of reality. Okay, let me put that in English. For example, for years we have heard that diet products are healthy, right? We diligently read the labels to see how many calories they contain, and how much fat, carbohydrates, and sugar we will be consuming. Everything looks in line, and so we begin substituting a diet bar or a protein shake for a meal. Have you ever wondered why we eat and drink so many low-calorie products and yet millions still suffer from obesity? Isn't it odd that you rarely see a thin person eating or drinking diet products?

Why do you suppose that is? Could it be that our perceptions about diet products need to change? Perhaps—just perhaps—diet products aren't that good for us, and the ingredients they contain have changed our bodily functions along with our mistaken reality that if we consume diet products, we'll lose weight? How can this be? After all, manufacturers have told us they are low-cal and sugar-free, and they featured all those thin people in their ads and television commercials.

Television commercials, ad campaigns, and friends and family members have repeatedly told us how healthy the diet products are, and the more we heard it, the more we believed it. So, not only did our bodily functions change but so did our perceptions and behaviors, which gave us a new reality—those diet products were healthy and would make us lose weight. That's the danger of negative manipulation; it can be so strong that it changes our entire belief system. When we allow another to alter our thinking, it can take a long time to return to our previous reality. That's the awesome power of manipulation. You have the power to change another's reality.

Is It Ever Right to Manipulate Another?

Absolutely! It's right to manipulate them when you have their best interest in mind. For example, if the one you love is slowly killing themselves with drugs and you know they need to stop, it's perfectly acceptable to use your power of manipulation to intervene and empower them to create a new positive reality. If you are on a team with co-workers who cannot agree on a future vision for the project and so nothing is getting done, you are well within your rights to practice a bit of sound manipulation. Everyone is better off if it helps the team get focused on the goal.

Practicing Manipulation Has Consequences and Obligations

Once you have learned how to manipulate others, you have a duty to only use that power in a positive way. If you decide to selfishly apply the skills you will learn in these five steps, there could be significant consequences that will negatively impact your life. Once you have manipulated a person's reality, you have an obligation to mentor and guide them as they explore and investigate their new perceptions and beliefs.

The bigger the changes in perceptions and behaviors, the more support will be needed. You are not using this NLP power of manipulation correctly if you persuade someone to move in a different direction and then abandon them when they need you the most. So, along with the powers of manipulation, you owe it to yourself and others to offer guidance and encouragement along the way. Should you unintentionally lead another on a negative path, then together you must set a new desired outcome and work with one another to achieve that desired result.

Some Are Easy to Manipulate--Some Are Not

You would think those who are easy to manipulate are always the ones who are meek and introverted, but this is not always the case. Often, the very people who think others could never manipulate them, are the easiest to influence and persuade. The seemingly stronger personalities are unsuspecting and unprepared. Because few people ever try to control those with more powerful personalities, they don't see the manipulative signals. Whereas, weaker people who experience manipulation frequently will recognize your attempts and might have built up more resistance.

It's important to remember that all of us experience manipulation every day. When you learn the five steps presented in our book, you'll quickly recognize when it's happening to you. Don't be surprised if you think you're manipulating a person when he or she is manipulating you. You see this frequently going on in close relationships, especially if one is a giver and the other a taker. The "giver" will give a little, and then a bit more—asking nothing in return, at first. The taker will enjoy the taking, and might even consider the fact that being in this relationship requires nothing of him or her. Ah, but not so fast!

Once the giver has obligated the "taker" by always being the one to give on the little things, there is a huge request made. The taker in the relationship now feels he or she has no choice but to comply after all the giver so rarely expects anything of them. Guess what? The taker, whom you would have thought was the manipulator, has now been manipulated.

What matters more than the personality type of person experiencing the manipulation is his or her motivation to change, desired outcome, and the strength of their previous programming. Some weak people play the victim, and the challenge to manipulate their thinking is almost insurmountable. Why? Because many individuals who act as victims are the ones who are manipulating you, and it's much harder to manipulate a manipulator.

Even though it would be more positive for them to get what they want by being empowered and encouraged to do so in a positive way, the victim is often too content in their role to transition to a place of power easily. They have created their reality, and that reality has made them a victim. We see this with people who have repeatedly been abused, beaten down, or experience constant drama. Manipulating them can be impossible because they are already getting their desired outcome. You'll understand more about this in a later chapter.

The five steps in this book will give you a roadmap of strategies and techniques that teach you to manipulate and persuade others to do what is best for them. The beauty of positive manipulation is that while helping others, you also help yourself. That's the way our world works. Some people call it Karma, but it is positive thoughts and actions attracting more positives. The same is true with negative manipulation; it draws more negative into your life and the lives of others, and so your reality will be one of loneliness and isolation when you selfishly manipulate others. After being manipulated by you for selfish gain, people won't want to be around you; you now have destroyed their trust. Coming back from that position is a long haul and one in which many never return to their former self.

What's the Difference Between Control and Manipulation?

The difference between the two is subtle, but there is a slight distinction. When you are attempting to control people, you make a suggestion to try to influence them, or out-and-out dictate to them what they will do because you have control. When you manipulate people, you arrange for them to share your experiences, and move them toward the behavior or belief that you wish them to have. You're not controlling them; you're demonstrating and explaining what is best for them, and doing so in a way that is more covert. It's that secret thing that makes all the difference. Many people can be manipulated but not controlled.

Individuals who are not good at manipulation don't achieve success because they are too outwardly controlling, and people resent that action. If used negatively, to hurt people, manipulation can be much more dangerous and lasting. The time factor is another difference between the two. When you control another's behavior, if you are no longer present to influence them constantly, it is hard to maintain that same control. Whereas, if you are manipulating people, they don't realize they are intentionally moved to think, behave, and believe in a particular manner. Because manipulation entirely changes one's perspective, they do not return to their old way of thinking as easily because you have helped them to create for themselves a new reality.

How Can You Tell When You Are Negatively Manipulated?

Don't waste your time trying to figure out IF you are experiencing manipulation—we are all shaped and managed to one extent or another. What you need to be aware of are the times' someone is trying to negatively manipulate you—to persuade or move you to do things that go against your personal values and boundaries. Here are ten ways to identify when you are the victim of negative manipulation.

1. Although you have changed your beliefs and behaviors, you have an underlying unrest about the new you.

2. You are obsessed with your new reality and talk about it all the time as if to justify why you believe and behave the way you do. However, when you try to describe why you think and act this way now, your explanations are weak and unsatisfying. You end up saying "Well, it's hard to explain," to others.

3. You often feel anxious, distrusting, jealous, or incompetent around your manipulator, especially if that person is someone with whom you are involved with romantically.

4. You have extreme mood swings, and your happiness is dependent upon the attitude of your manipulator.

5. You hold your manipulator in such high regard and feel as though you are betraying him or her if you should dare to disagree.

6. You have a lower self-esteem unless your manipulator is there to boost your spirit.

7. You are more guarded in your words and actions. You do this because manipulators frequently withdraw their friendship or affections from you when you have said or done something that is contrary to what they believe or how they behave.

8. It seems like you can never do anything right, and you find yourself apologizing all the time.

9. Your primary purpose is to make your manipulator happy, and you find yourself sacrificing your happiness for his or hers.

10. You become more isolated from your former friends and find that your social life is almost non-existent except for that of your manipulator.

Although these feelings and behaviors would only happen in the most extreme cases, you might experience several at once in a new friendship or relationship. It never hurts to keep your eyes and ears open to the fact that manipulation occurs all around us. Some of it is an attempt to persuade us to a different reality that is so much better than that in which we leave behind. However, some manipulators are only out for what will benefit themselves, and it matters not who gets caught in the crossfire. If they can use you to get what they want, you become the next rung on their ladder to success.

If you should recognize some of these ten signs that indicate negative manipulation, challenge your manipulator and observe his or her response. Standing up for yourself is better done sooner than later because once the manipulation continues for a long time, those manipulated begin to stop questioning and merely accept their new reality. They are the lemmings in this life, the zombies who walk about with feelings so buried they no longer have a sense of self. They are tossed about from one manipulator to another because they have changed their reality so many times they no longer have ownership in their lives.

In the following chapters, you will get insight into manipulation, mind control, and how to use NLP in a positive manner. So, here's to helping you change your perspective about manipulation and perhaps empower you to create a new reality of getting more of what you want and helping others to do the same.

Chapter 2: Step #1—Building Rapport vs. Fear

To practice positive manipulation, it's necessary to build rapport rather than strike fear in the minds of those you are manipulating. Not that fear won't do the job, but it's a harmful practice that will end up coming back to bite you in the behind. Contrary manipulators create fear in the minds of others, then play the hero, and immediately remove the fear with their manipulation. Fear is such a strong emotion that it quickly opens the doors of the mind for manipulation or mind control; however, the problem lies in the after effects. Fear doesn't necessarily allow you to change people's perspective and behavior; it is more of a short, immediate reaction that goes away once there's no longer any fear. Their reality hasn't changed. The old practices and behaviors are still lurking just below the surface—ready to resurface as soon as you alleviate the fear.

When you use fear to manipulate beliefs or behaviors, you don't create a long-lasting change in that person's reality. What you just might create is a long-term distrust. The people you are trying to manipulate will begin to associate you with their feelings of fear. Make no mistake, fear is one of the most powerful and efficient ways to manage people, and its results are immediate. The fortunate thing is that people who behave in a certain way out of fear, usually avoid the person and thereby the fear as well.

Results from Using the Fear Strategy to Manipulate

Since childhood, most of us have experienced fear manipulation. Our parents manipulated and controlled us by physical discipline or emotional blackmail, and our teachers managed us by threats and humiliation. Unfortunately, our perspectives and beliefs weren't changed at all, only our behaviors—and those changed only temporarily. What many learned by the time they were teenagers is that they didn't want to be around parents and teachers, and the friends or peers whose realities were similar became our closest network with the greatest amount of influence over them.

To illustrate this point, let's look at Raul. Raul entered the tenth-grade with a reputation for being a trouble-maker. He harassed all the girls in class, destroyed the classroom desks and books, and disrespected his teachers. When Raul tried his usual tactics with his English teacher, Miss Slater, she decided to call his father. Expecting that Raul's father would offer his support, she never dreamed he'd come down to the school and humiliate Raul in front of all his friends.

Unfortunately, Raul had to sit next to his father all day long as his father accompanied him to every class, pulling him by the ear from one room to another. Did it put the fear of God in him? I'm sure it did. Unfortunately, when the fear factor no longer held him hostage, Raul's behavior was even more disrespectful and threatening than before. He still harassed the girls in class, but now he warned them if they told he would meet them outside the classroom and make them sorry. What Raul's father had taught him was to manipulate through fear. Because Raul didn't experience positive manipulation, his reality was the same—act out and get all the attention you want. Since negative attention was all the attention Raul every experienced, he knew no better.

Not only did he continue to disrespect the girls in class, but he covertly sabotaged his teachers with practical jokes that were destructive and dangerous. He blew his nose and wiped the discharge between the pages of brand new textbooks. He keyed his teacher's car, and one day he sucked in the fumes from a butane lighter and blew them out as he lighted his breath. The fire was like a torch, catching the girl's hair on fire who sat in front of him. Instead of changing his behavior, practicing manipulation through fear hurt others and got him permanently expelled from school for the remainder of the year.

Comparing Fear Manipulation to Positive Rapport-Building Manipulative Attempts

The next year Raul returned, along with his reputation for being a rebellious bully. By now, his reality was "get them before they get me" school of thought. The fear manipulation hadn't achieved any beneficial changes in Raul's behaviors or perspective, except to reinforce the negative. What made matters worse is he was now a year behind his classmates and in danger of becoming another dropout statistic.

Fortunately for Raul, he got more than he bargained for in one of his new teachers, Mr. Thompson. Mr. Thompson was obviously a teacher who realized how to move and empower his students through positive manipulation; thereby, helping them to create a new reality for themselves. Raul came into the classroom with the same old mean-spirited, sour attitude, but instead of a write-up, after the reprimand, after another write-up, what Raul experienced was a teacher who believed in teaching through the continuous power of healthy relationships.

One day, both were in detention—Raul for disciplinary reasons from another hard-nosed teacher, and Mr. Thompson to act as supervisor for after-school detention. Mr. Thompson had a whole week of after-school detention time to build rapport with Raul. Mr. Thompson questioned Raul about his likes and dislikes, only to discover Raul's love for fast cars. Since Mr. Thompson's hobby was rebuilding an old muscle-car he had inherited from his great aunt, he decided to involve Raul in the process. He brought the car to school and stored it in the industrial arts building. Every day after school, Mr. Thompson and Raul would work on the car together.

Through his questions and rapport building, Mr. Thompson manipulated Raul to change his "get them before they get me" perspective on life. The improved behavior that began in Mr. Thompson's class soon spread to other aspects of Raul's life as well. As they finished the car, Mr. Thompson permitted Raul the privilege of taking dates out in his amazing muscle car. Girls had a new respect for Raul and his disrespectful attitude changed for them as well. Raul's mechanical talents surpassed that of Mr. Thompson, and he was often called to the house to assist him with needed repairs, strengthening their friendship and mutual respect.

Although it was a challenge to catch up, Raul passed that year with flying colors. As the years passed, he grew more confident and changed from rebellious to productive. His grades were good, and it was evident Raul had a real talent to repair anything mechanical. Toward the end of his senior year, Raul talked to Mr. Thompson about his inability to afford college and together they discussed other employment options. Graduation night, Raul had the biggest smile of any other student as he collected his diploma, knowing how hard he had worked and how many obstacles he had overcome with Mr. Thompson's help.

His mother and father had since divorced, and Raul's mom and younger brother were the only ones who cheered him on that evening. He searched the crowd for Mr. Thompson's familiar cheery face but was disappointed when he failed to see him in the line of teachers wishing their students good luck in their future endeavors. It was difficult for Raul to hid his disappointment as he slowly led his mother and brother down the front steps and out to the parking lot.

Raul felt so sorry for himself that he didn't see the bright red, 1965, convertible Mustang GTX at first until his mother touched his arm and spoke in a tearful voice. "Raul, I think Mr. Thompson has a surprise for you."

"I looked for him, but..."

"He's right there with your present."

There parked right in front of the steps was the car they had worked on for two years. It had a huge gold ribbon around it, with the words "Class of 1999" written on the window. Mr. Thompson was there to hand Raul the keys and wish him good luck in his future endeavors.

Today Raul owns a body shop, helps to support his mother and pays for his brother to attend the local junior college. That's the power of positive manipulation and Step #1 in our five steps.

Step #1—Building Rapport

It's a proven fact that people will do what you ask if you use fear or negative manipulation, but the real change happens when you build rapport and a positive relationship with them. That's what Mr. Thompson did with Raul. Let's look at how he manipulated Raul into changing his thinking, his perspective, his behaviors, and then helped him to create a new reality.

1. Discover Common Ground

   Mr. Thompson took the time to discover Raul's passion in life. What was it that got him excited? What would turn him on and plug him into life? At first, Raul spoke sarcastically about negative things, but he finally mentioned his love for fast cars. Here was something that Raul and Mr. Thompson had in common. Easy conversation not Raul's first response to Mr. Thompson's questions; it took some digging to find some common ground in which Mr. Thompson could begin to manipulate Raul to move in another direction positively.

   So, asking questions is necessary to find the first building-block of rapport, and it takes rapport to establish substantial grounds for manipulation.

2. Change the Focus

   Instead of harping on Raul about his bad behavior or poor grades, Mr. Thompson began to talk about cars with Raul. Soon, Raul turned his focus from belligerently spouting off about things he hated to calming discussing things he felt passionate about with Mr. Thompson. Bottom line, Mr. Thompson manipulated Raul to change his emotional state from negative to positive, and in doing so, he got Raul to begin thinking about positive outcomes resulting from his changed behaviors. If Raul worked hard and got the car running—if he performed well in school—if he were more respectful to girls, then he would get to drive the car he helped to rebuild. Instead of focusing on what he couldn't do, Raul began to measure his new reality by what he could do.

3. Approval and Acceptance

   Whenever Mr. Thompson showed approval and acceptance of Raul's behavior, it strengthened the young man's resolve to continue along that same path. Raul began to enjoy the positive attention, praise, and encouragement. Not only did he meet Mr.

Thompson's expectations, but Raul exceeded them. His previous reality of "get them before they get me," was now changing to "do more for them than they do for me."

4. Reinforce the New Behavior

Mr. Thompson then continued the positive manipulation by reinforcing Raul's budding new reality. They made an agreement; if Raul continued to do well in school and be respectful, he could take his dates out in the Mustang. What a thrill it was for Raul. For the first time, Raul got more attention from being respectful than he did from being physically and emotionally abusive. The better he behaved, the more positive reinforcement he received.

5. Reward the Change

Most of us think of Raul's big prize as the Mustang, but that was not the final win. What changed Raul's reality for life was all the positive he brought to others from his changed perspective and behavior. Appreciation and thanks from his brother and mother were Raul's continued rewards. The business Raul built as a result of all his hard work was a reward. Mr. Thompson's positive manipulation that created an entirely new reality and offered him a future he could never have imagined possible was Raul's final prize.

These are the five components of Step #1—Building Rapport vs. fear. Fear manipulation changed nothing for Raul, but positive manipulation through building rapport changed his life. Not only was Raul rewarded, but Mr. Thompson's life was changed for the better as well. He and Raul remained good friends, and he learned the difference a teacher could make in the life of a young person. He learned exceptional manipulation skills that he still practices today to move his students to peak performance in the classroom and life.

Chapter 3: Step #2—Defining Desired Outcomes

I'm sure you've heard that the best negotiations are a win/win for everyone, right? Well, the same holds true for manipulation. The more valid form of manipulations is in which everybody wins. It's like a good relationship; if one person does all the taking and another all the giving, the relationship isn't going to last. When practicing the most efficient and effective forms of manipulation, if both parties don't feel as though they benefited, the desired outcome will not be achieved. To know what it will take to make you and the other person feel like winners, you need to know what you want and what they want.

What Do You Want for Your Desired Outcome?

If you don't define your desired outcomes, how will you know when you have achieved your goals and helped them to accomplish theirs as well? As important as it was to ask your subject questions to build rapport, it's just as important to ask yourself questions to determine what you want. The following are some suggested questions that will help you identify your desired outcome. If you think you know what your desired outcome is, question further to determine if this is your passionate desire.

For illustration purposes, let's imagine that your desired outcome was to lead the top-performing team in your workplace. However, to achieve this desired result, you need buy-in from the other team members. First, test your stated desired outcome to make sure it is your passion. If you are not passionate about your desired outcome, you cannot manipulate others to your way of thinking and behaving. Your team may do well, but your reality of leading the top performing team at work will probably not happen. The following questions will enable you to test your level of passion.

1. How will leading the top performing team in my workplace change my reality?

2. What will I experience in this changed reality that I cannot experience now?

3. What will I need to do to make my desired outcome a reality?

4. Am I willing to do what was listed in #3 to attain my desired result?

5. How will the rest of my team benefit when I manipulate them to my way of thinking?

Once you have successfully examined the answers to these questions, and everything still points to a win/win for everyone involved, you're ready to begin your manipulations to move the other team members to greater production and performance.

What Desired Outcomes Do You Want for Those You are Manipulating?

There's only one thing you want for them, and that is for them to benefit from doing what you want them to do. You already know what you need the subject of your manipulations to do, how to think and behave, and now what you want for them is to jump on board. The problem is, they're less likely to be manipulated to your way of thinking if it doesn't turn them on, if they cannot relate to your desired outcome, or if they are not passionate about what you want for them.

Let's face it, you know they would be better off if their work performance was top-notch. You know all team players would feel better about themselves and be more likely to be promoted or receive bonuses if they were members of the top performing team, right? And, that is your desired outcome for you and them. Now, what you must do is determine what gives each one an immediate payoff to persuade them to seek that position as top performing team. It's the instant gratification that will get the team's attention and manipulate them to participate in your desired outcome.

That's where the rapport building skills come in handy. You need to build rapport with every member of your team and discover what each person's payoff will be before they are "all in" to move toward your desired outcome. Don't think it's always going to be money, either. Here are some primary motivators that manipulators use to move people to their desired outcome.

- Friendship
- Recognition
- Power
- Wealth
- Position
- Praise
- Belonging
- Material Possessions
- Fame
- Prestige
- Envy of Others
- Help Family
- For the Fun
- Challenge
- Emotional and Physical Well-Being

Making Your Manipulation All About Others

Manipulation is entirely different from convincing people on your ideas. People don't want you to "sell" them on your desired outcome; they want to attain their desired outcome through their individual ideas and efforts. What needs to happen for long-term manipulation to occur is that others have total buy-in to your desired outcome. In fact, before completing your manipulations, your desired outcome and theirs should be the same. That's a real reality change that will last the test of time.

Think of the wants and needs of those whom you are manipulating as your hook to get their attention and real them in to come to your desired outcome. It is still done in a positive manner—not by fear, intimidation, or humiliation. Using the same example of the team of co-workers, let's examine the five things you can do to get them to help you achieve your desired outcome and still reward them for their efforts.

1. Instead of focusing on what they are doing wrong, focus on what you are doing right. Talk about how rewarding it has been to be privileged enough to lead the group and how you plan to make the team the top-performers in the company. State your desired outcome as a team effort. Include them in your plans for the entire team to be successful. Praise them, perhaps telling them that you are happy you are a part of their team. They are hand-chosen for success. Of course, this is also true for other situations of manipulations. Always involve the ones you are manipulating with your plans of success.

2. Model the behavior and beliefs you wish them to have to achieve your desired outcome. It does little good to expect others to participate in your desired outcome if you don't give it your all as well. Those you want to manipulate will want to please you, so make sure you are modeling the behavior and perceptions you want from them. If you expect them to give it 150 percent, then you do the same. If you expect your team members to work until the project gets done, then you be there right along with them.

   If this is not a work project, but someone with whom you are in a relationship with that you wish to manipulate, then you must model your expectations. If you want them to listen to you, then you must be willing to hear them as well. If you want them to be more responsive to your needs, then you need to be more sensitive to their needs. That's the way everybody wins—everybody benefits from your desired outcome.

3. Assume all members are already on board with your ideas. Assumptions are an essential element to manipulating others. Don't ask for their opinions or ideas, believe theirs is the same as yours. If someone expresses an opposing view, let them know you value their input, and their concerns are quite insightful. Then, explain how those very concerns are addressed with your plan. Gain acceptance and approval by encouraging them to state how they have already benefited from the changes that have taken place. If you become a dictator and tell someone what to think, they can always deny or doubt the validity of what you say. However, if you manipulate the situation in a way that convinces them to

state their agreement, then those you are manipulating are not going to doubt their stated beliefs.

4. Talk and act as if you are already the top performing team in the company. The more you do, the more your team members will adopt this attitude as well. If you want to manipulate someone into being more responsible, give them more trust and let them prove their responsibility. If people want to have more privileges, then they should demonstrate responsibility first. What about you? Do you believe this statement? In truth, the reverse is true. If you want people to be more accountable, give them more privileges and let them demonstrate their responsibility.

Do you hear how the two views are slightly different? I'm sure you've heard parents say to their children "You disobeyed me; there will be no more privileges until you can earn back my trust." Really? How can that happen when the child has little opportunity to do so? In our reality, things happen just the other way around. Okay, we're going to give you this privilege, and "assume" you will be trustworthy.

5. When you have observed a team-member going above and beyond the others, give plenty of public recognition and praise. Soon, others on the team will want the same for themselves. Everybody likes to be valued and appreciated.

There was a young mother who always complained that her son wouldn't do his chores, and when he did decide to do some work around the house it was never right, and he still wanted to get paid his allowance. Until she learned how to manipulate his behavior and perceptions, her son continued to display a rather lazy attitude with the unreasonable expectations of being paid for nothing.

So, how did she manipulate her son into defining a new reality? First, she asked and expected nothing of him. His younger brother continued to do his chores, was given praise and recognition, and paid his usual allowance in front of his older brother at the end of the week. The mother showed affection to her older son as well, but he was not praised or recognized for chores that he had not done. She would mention her younger son's achievements to the father as he came home from work, and the father would also acknowledge the younger brother's good behavior in the presence of his older son. Nothing negative was said or done to punish the older child, but there was no display of pleasure for work he did not do.

In just over a week, the older son wanted in on the positive rewards, as well as the allowance. He eagerly completed his daily chores and did a good job. The mother's desired outcome for her son was for him to do his chores without complaining, and do them to her standards. She also made an agreement with her oldest son that she would not nag him to do his chores; it was his choice. If he wanted his allowance, then the assigned tasks would need to be done.

The surprise in her manipulation was when she had forgotten to give her son his allowance, and he had forgotten to ask for it. His beliefs, behaviors, and perspective had changed so drastically that his motivation was no longer the money, but the reward was the recognition and praise. The beauty of positive manipulation is that everybody wins.

Manipulation Takes Consistency, Control, and Focus

The more challenging the desired outcome for you and others, the more consistency, control and focus it requires from the manipulator. Remember, you need to model the behavior. Passion and patience are necessary to achieve your goal and help others change their reality to align with your desires. Modeling your outcome needs to be an exaggeration of what you want others to do. For example, let's say your desired outcome is for there to be no swearing or yelling in your home. You don't' want your husband or children to swear—not one word. You don't even want your company and friends to curse when they are visiting.

The obvious first step is to let everybody know that you would like your home to be a swear-free zone. Next, you are the first one to clean up your language. That means no swearing by you in the presence of your husband or children, or even when you think they can't hear you. No swearing. Next, you let them know how much calmer you feel when you're not resorting to swearing. Assume you hear no swearing, and comment on how good it feels not to let frustration get the best of you.

Every time you want to swear but resist the temptation, give a little giggle and say how you're not going to swear. Cheerfully comment on how good it is not to let your immature emotions get the best of you. When you notice less swearing in the house, you praise your family on controlling their language. To continue the manipulation, mention how much happier everybody is with less swearing and verbal frustration in the house. When someone uses a substitute word where they would have previously sworn, make a joke of it and let them know how clever they are to have thought of using that word.

Point out the peacefulness and calm you feel, and how grown up it is to see your children control their frustration and emotions. Don't be surprised if your children's friends swear in the house and you don't have to correct them. You've done such a good job manipulating your kids that they'll admonish their friends for the swearing and let them know your home is now a swear-free zone.

All this fuss over swearing might seem silly to many of you, but it's a way to practice your manipulation methods. Try manipulation on smaller things first, and then move on to bigger issues when you have honed your skills. Be sure that you are just as passionate about the desired outcomes on the smaller things, or you won't be successful. Your passion for changing other's reality is what drives you to achieve the desired results.

Chapter 4: Step #3—Considering the Consequences

Every action has a consequence, whether you choose to accept it or not. We are all so connected, that what you do directly affects the behaviors and actions of others. There is no better reason to act and behave responsibly regarding manipulation. If you do believe that we are connected, then should you choose to manipulate another in a negative way, you are bringing all the negative consequences right back on yourself. For this reason, you must consider the consequences of your behaviors and decisions when you are manipulating others. Step #3 is one of the most important ones to reaching your desired outcome.

If you have done your homework before manipulating others, you are acutely aware of the first consequence of your actions. Most of you have researched and weighed what you want that desired outcome to be, and you prepare yourself for the consequences of your actions. However, what surprises you is that most manipulative activities have secondary effects that may not evolve until much later. The secondary effects seem to happen so randomly that you fail to connect these new behaviors or beliefs with your original action.

The United States unemployment benefits is an excellent example of delayed consequences that nobody considered would be the direct result of manipulation. Originally designed to help people who had lost their jobs or were out of work for a short period, unemployment, the government intervened and offered compensation until people could re-train themselves and get back on their feet. While this worked in the beginning, the result we see in our current society is not quite so positive. Many of today's workers have learned how to manipulate the system, creating a reality that is not quite what the government had counted on happening. Instead of unemployment compensation helping people who are out of work, it has held them back from returning to the workforce and becoming productive citizens.

Instead of collecting unemployment for a short period while they are actively seeking a job, many people discover how long they can receive the benefits to which they feel entitled. Instead of trying to find a job immediately, they live off unemployment pay until it is down to zero. However, the secondary consequences continue even further. With these unemployed workers' prolonged absences from the workplace, different skills, and systems progress. Now they are no longer qualified or knowledgeable enough to compete with their peers. The money has run out, so they can no longer collect unemployment benefits at a time when they need the financial help.

What happens now is an endless cycle of governmental handouts, which was not a part of the government's desired outcomes? The unemployed soon move from unemployment benefits to Welfare, which was also only designed to help in a temporary capacity. The unintended consequences of these programs are that we now have generations of family members whose new reality is one where they were born and had lived most of their lives surviving the only way they know how—on Welfare. Although it was not the intent of the program, life-long Welfare recipients are cheated out of significant accomplishments because they grew up in a broken system as a result of unintentional consequences.

Nothing Comes without a Cost

When you decide to manipulate others, you must take responsibility for the new reality you help to create. If that reality wasn't quite what you bargained for, then the problem might have been that you didn't carefully consider the consequences of your actions. Here are some questions to ask yourself when thinking through the consequences that could occur because of your manipulations.

1. What will happen to myself and others if I manipulate this person?
2. What will happen to myself and others if I choose not to manipulate this person?
3. If I do nothing to manipulate the desired outcome, what happens?
4. If I do nothing to manipulate the outcome you want, what will not occur?
5. Will I and others be harmed if I do not manipulate the desired outcome?
6. Will I and others benefit from my manipulations?

7. Knowing there will be a cost, am I willing to take full responsibility for my manipulations?

8. Knowing that I could have positively affected the desired outcome, am I willing to take full liability for choosing not to manipulate the situation?

If everything comes with a cost, that means doing nothing also has its consequences. If you decide not to manipulate others, it might mean that you will not achieve your desired outcomes and nor will they. Are you willing to accept the consequences if you say no to the benefits that could happen if you were ready to follow the steps in this book and positively manipulate the other person? If you are still stuck on the belief that manipulating others is wrong, then you need to change your perception which will result in a new reality. Once you learn that manipulation can be rewarding, you'll wonder why you ever thought differently.

Accepting the Consequences is Empowering

Knowing that your actions and decisions have a profound effect on yourself and others is quite empowering. When you accept this reality, you are aware that you are in control of your destiny. If you want to manipulate your reality, then act and make that change happen. If you want to help others create a new reality, then you have the power to manipulate that situation to bring about for them a more positive desired outcome and a new reality that leads them to a better life. Knowing these truths about manipulation encourages you never to use manipulation to harm others because you would ultimately be doing harm to yourself and negatively change your reality as well.

Realizing the difference one person can make in the lives of many is a daunting consideration. Along with that come the "what if" concerns, such as "What if I make a mistake in my decision to manipulate?" Or, "What if the desired outcome is far from what I counted on and it hurts others?" These are real concerns, and you're right to play the "what if" game. If you learn to manipulate others, you are going to experience the consequences of bad decisions or poorly planned manipulation. There will be a time when someone gets hurt by your manipulations or a time when you don't achieve your desired outcome.

Nothing ventured—nothing gained is a rule that many manipulators adopt to be in charge of their future. If they decide never to manipulate others, then they will not experience all the benefits manipulation offers. What's worse, those who could have benefited will also lose the opportunity for a better life. All because you let fear stop you.

There's something about the fear you should know! You fear what you don't understand—what you don't know. It's natural to fear manipulation. First, you already have some preconceived ideas that perhaps aren't so positive about manipulation, so you've built the wall that you'll now have to scale. If you are empowered enough to create a whole new reality for yourself, you can also create enough fear to block success. It sounds perverse, but your fear of manipulation is manipulating you.

Fear is a self-imposed false belief, so your fearful reality is based on false facts. Decisions based on a false premise are not sound. That's why Step #1 in this book was about getting rid of the fear. You can't expect others to follow you if you fear the outcome. Chances are, the consequences you might experience from a poor decision are much lighter than the results you live now because you're bowing down to fear. It's not that you will never be fearful to move forward, but being an outstanding manipulator means you confidently pursue your desired result no matter what. If you begin manipulations with a wishy-washy belief, and your behaviors are On-again/off-again, your manipulations will fail. You'll disappoint those you want to help. Instead of letting the fear paralyze you, learn to push past it and scale that wall to a favorable desired result.

When Your Manipulations Aren't Working

Don't wait until the cows come home to change things up a little bit. When your efforts are coming to a stalemate, make some minor adjustments to your plan of action. The fact is when you begin manipulating others it doesn't seem like a very positive experience. The more others have been programmed to believe and behave in a particular way, the more resistant they are and the less ground you can cover. For a while, you might try making a few little changes.

Nothing major, just some small adjustments to your behaviors. If several minor changes in your plan don't create marked progress in your manipulation, it's time to shake things up with a radical change.

Making a radical change to force another's hand will usually accomplish one of two outcomes. Either you lose the opportunity to manipulate the other person, which you probably would have done anyway without a radical change; or, you will shake them out of their rut, and they'll begin moving forward to your desired outcome. Making a radical change acts as a wake-up call to those you are manipulating. It's like dumping ice water on the face of a sleeping person. You're going to wake them up for sure, and then they have a decision to make. Do they go for you, or do they laugh it off and start their day? At this point, it can go either way. What won't happen is another unproductive day where your manipulation goes nowhere, and your desired outcome gets further away until it seems to be out of reach.

Learning to Manipulate Is Not for the Faint of Heart

It takes courage to manage others. After all, you're the one taking risks, putting your reputation on the line, and leading another person or group to a better life. It's a battle of wills, and leaders in combat are the first to be injured if their plan of attack is flawed. On the other hand, leaders also reap the highest rewards. There's nothing like manipulating a situation where you get what you want, others get what they want, and you were directly responsible for the accomplishment. It's even better when others recognize you as the one who made it all happen, so don't be shy about tooting your own horn. It's a great way to set yourself up for the next time you need to manipulate the situation. Everybody likes to follow a proven winner.

If you're feeling fearful, don't give up because you think you don't have the courage to continue. Brave manipulators feel fear, they feel defeated, and they feel like giving up, but the difference is they don't give into their fears. They continue to do what they know will bring them greater opportunities for success. They continue to move people to do the same with their lives, even when the odds are against them.

Chapter 5: Step #4—Be the Solution to their Problem

It's difficult to manipulate people when they don't feel there is a need for change. Creating that need is paramount in your ability to control and manage the situation and get what you want. The people you want to manipulate always have needs and wants, so it's up to you to discover their needs and then prove to them you are the answer. Instead of thinking of what they want as a need, consider that need to be a problem. It's either a problem they have or a problem caused by what they don't have.

I can hear the wheels turning in your head about right now. You're probably saying to yourself, but what if their need isn't a real problem? Don't go there; think of it as a problem, and it will make your manipulation easier to set up, even if the problem is a good one to have.

To demonstrate this method, let's create a scenario where you are a real estate agent, and you want to manipulate your prospects into purchasing a home. The prospects visit your community, and the exchange goes something like this.

Step #1—Building Rapport

Remember, you cannot manipulate until you have built rapport, so here are some of the things you'll want to do to build rapport.

- Smile and get up out of your chair to greet them.
  There's nothing worse when you're visiting a new home community to have someone sitting in their office who's too lazy to greet you and thank you for coming in to see them. Waving them through to the models is more likely to build an enemy than a friend.

- Next, you'll introduce yourself and get their name.

It might sound something like this as you offer your hand. "Hi, my name is Linda—and you are...?" Most people will tell you their names. If they don't tell you their names then you can always say: "I'm so bad with names. What did you say your first name was?" Do this after you've made some small talk and gained their trust.

Continue to make casual conversation until the prospects relax. If you can get them to laugh, you're well on your way. Once you have learned their names, use them. Everybody likes to hear their name. Not too much or it will sound manipulative, just pepper the conversation here and there with their names.

Step #2—Defining Desired Outcomes

During Step #2, you'll be asking lots of questions to discover what they want. Of course, when you ask them what they are looking for in a new home, the standard answer will be "Well, we need a three bedroom, two-bath home." Since that's not very enticing, and you know that's the standard answer, you might come back with a laugh and say, "Okay, soooo—let me get this straight. If I have a three bedroom, two-bath home to sell you today, you'll be ready to buy, right?"

Of course, they are going to laugh at you, and then you begin to dig a little more. To discover the reason the prospects are out looking for a new home, you continue to ask more questions that make them think a little. It might sound like this: "So, Joan, when you and Ken were sitting over dinner talking about the new home you would love to own, how did that home look? If this were your perfect dream home, what would it look like?" Now you've got them thinking; they're more engaged in the conversation.

Step #3—Considering the Consequences

On this next step in your attempts to manipulate the prospects, you engage their imagination and help them to see the consequences of their decision. What would their life be like if they moved, or what would their life be like if they decided not to move? When you engage a person's imagination, don't be afraid to ask them to play along. It might sound like this. "Joan and Ken, I'm going to ask you to pretend with me for a moment. If you decided not to purchase a home and instead stay in the home you are currently living in, what would your life be like—let's say, for the next year?"

You always want to put a timeframe on that question to keep them focused on the immediacy or urgency of their decision. Now is when you're going to get to the "problem." Let's say your prospects said something like this. "Well, it would be difficult for us to stay in our current home because we just found out Joan is pregnant and we're going to need more space. Okay, that's a problem, but it's still going to take some more questions to determine whether this is the most pressing issue, or if there is another underlying issue.

For example, the prospects might need more space as well, but the real problem might be that they don't want to raise their child in that neighborhood, or in that school district. Whatever the issue may be, it might take some more flushing out with continued questioning. It's common that people don't disclose their problem early on in a relationship. They need time to develop trust.

Okay, let's say the real problem was that they need more space for their growing family. What you need to do in your manipulations now, is to expand the problem. Blow it way out of proportion, as if you were blowing up a balloon. Your next questions might be as follows:

- "Do you have enough property to add another bedroom onto your current home?"
  (Let's say they cannot add another bedroom.)

- "So, if you were to stay in your current home for the next year, what would your life be like?"
  (The prospects begin to tell you how difficult it would be to grow their family and stay in this tiny home.)

- Now, comes more manipulation. Remember when we discussed that you cannot dictate or tell a person what they need because they will doubt it when YOU say it? It's critical at this point to get the prospects to say they need to purchase a home, and that's so much easier than what you could imagine. All you need to do is ask this one little question and frame it this way.

"So, if you have no space to add a bedroom, and you are going to need the extra room, or it's going to be difficult to get around in your tiny house, what is it that you need to do?" After you ask this question, you stop talking. The next thing that happens is the prospects give you the answer you want to hear. They say, "Well, I guess we'll need to make a move."

Once you've manipulated the conversation and got the prospects to see their need or "problem," all you must to do is be the solution to their problem. The manipulation was getting the people to say what you wanted to hear. As in every plan, you know what success will look and sound like, so you need to move the person into ownership of their problem. They must voice what you want as if it were their idea.

Step #4—Be the Solution to their Problem

The reason I went through the first three steps before discussing Step #4 is so that you could see the manipulation sequence. It is easier to follow when you see the progression of your manipulation. When you are manipulating the person to see you as the solution to their problem, you must show them how you and your ideas or plan or perceptions are superior to anyone else's. What makes you stand out from the crowd? To give yourself that notable difference and your manipulation a winning boost, you need to listen to what they say they want and observe their responses to your probing questions. When they look excited about something you've said, file that in your memory. If they seem agitated when you are probing for more information, keep in mind what you were discussing when they showed their discomfort.

Being smart about how you set yourself apart will help you manipulate the people or situation and get what you want while helping them also achieve their goal. If what you are proposing doesn't help them solve their problem, then you haven't succeeded. You haven't reached your desired outcome. Instead of being the solution to their problem, you may have created a whole other issue. Even if you are the solution to their problem, but you haven't made yourself indispensable, then they won't recognize you as having the solution.

There could be many ways to solve their problem, but your manipulations should convince them that your way is the best way. You don't have to prove that you have the solution, all you need to do is manipulate their perception. The idea that you are the solution to their problem is merely a mindset. People believe what they want to believe, so your job is to make them want to believe in you. If you've had success with the other three steps, then coming to an agreement that you have the solution is just the natural culmination of your manipulation.

Empathetic Manipulation

Empathetic manipulation is a gray area because it is so easy to play upon one's emotions, which can move you into selfish and negative manipulation that is designed to benefit nobody but yourself. Remember what we said about this type of manipulation? In the end, everybody loses, including you. If you use empathetic manipulation to the detriment of others, you will eventually lose their trust and friendship. Having said this, if you decide to be empathetic when you are manipulating others, do so with caution. A little goes a long way.

In the case of the new homes salesperson, he or she could safely let the prospects know their problem was common and he would help them find a solution, but to display false emotions or deep caring that isn't real is taking unfair advantage. If you pretend to be the solution to their problem when, in fact, you know you are not, your manipulation will fail or be only a brief blip on the screen of their reality. Not only that, but this kind of pretense is often transparent, even to the most naïve.

Knowing that people make decisions emotionally and justify them logically, it's important that you identify and understand the emotions they feel. However, it is harmful manipulation when you prey upon their emotions to get them to follow you like little zombies. If you have real empathy for them, your manipulations will be fair and just. You can show your compassion by being understanding and then continue to manipulate them if you know it will be to their benefit. Unfortunately, if during the time of managing them you discover something that you know will hurt them if you continue, it's time to stop. Manipulations over!

Chapter 6: Step #5—Assuming Success

You may think your focus is on success, but it could be of worry and anxiety about not getting what you want. Studies have shown that people who focus on what they want are more likely to achieve their goals. However, the focus must be on what you want, not what you don't want. Although that sounds easy enough, let's illustrate the difference. Pretend your significant other has a cold, and you don't want to catch it. You believe in the power of positive thought and affirmations, so your plan is to focus on not getting a cold. Several times a day you say to yourself "I will not catch this cold. I will not catch this cold."

Here's the problem. This mindset or perspective is just the opposite of where you should focus. Instead of focusing on good health, you're focused on the cold. If you want to practice positive affirmations, what you should be saying to yourself is "I am healthy and vigorous. I am healthy, active, and full of energy." See the difference? One statement keeps your mind centered on the cold, while the other keeps you focused on good health and an active body. The reason positive affirmations don't work for a lot of people is that the affirmations aren't so positive.

The Strongest Voice in your Life is Your Own

The best way to analyze if you are assuming success and focusing on the positive is to analyze your self-talk. What does that little voice in your head say to you all the time? Have you been positively focused on achieving your desired outcome, or does your self-talk sound something like this: "I don't want my son to take drugs anymore." Or, "I want to stop smoking and have the rest of my family quit as well." What is your mind focused on right now? Smoking, right?

How can you manipulate your thoughts to change your focus and achieve your desired outcome? The quickest way is to change your self-talk to this. "I eat healthily, drink plenty of water, watch what I put in my mouth, and have clear lungs." Instead of smoking, your focus is on being healthy.

Translating this to assuming success, you need to examine your self-talk during the times you are moving forward to achieve your desired outcome. Let's pretend you want your husband to stop using the credit card so much and get it paid down to zero. You've given it lots of thought, and you focus on being out of debt. You have talked to your husband about your desires and asked him not to use the credit card. You've even tried to manipulate the situation through praise and reward for not using the card. You've heard about the power of visualization, so you've visualized the amount on your credit card getting lower and lower each day. Okay, now here's my question. How would you feel if that's what happened—if you paid the credit card in full? Would you be pleasantly surprised?

I hope you got the issues with this way of thinking. Let's look at your focus.

1. You imagined your husband not using the credit card instead of imagining a wallet full of cash to pay for your wanted items. Even though you stated you wanted your husband to stop using the credit card, your focus was still on the card.

2. You next said that your focus would be to get out of debt. Still, instead of an emphasis on a positive cash flow and all the money you have in the bank, your focus is on your debt. You have assumed debt to be in your future.

3. You then pass on your negative focus on not using the credit card to your husband, and his thoughts fuel the fire. Why? Because now you have two minds concentrated on the credit card. Praise and reward were even given to strengthen your thinking about the credit card.

4. Now you visualize the amount on the credit card getting lower, instead of your cash flow getting stronger.

5. When asked how you would feel if that happened, did you catch the most important word in the sentence? It was the elephant in the room—the "IF." If you were assuming success that word would have been "WHEN" not "IF."

6. Lastly, when asked if you were pleasantly surprised--if you always assume success there should never be a surprise when getting what you want. Your success was no accident—it was the achievement of a chosen desired outcome.

There has been much discussion on manipulating others to change their perspective, but before you can do that, you might need to change your thinking as well. Always assume success. Every thought you have should lead you to your desired outcome. Every word spoken should focus your mind on what you want. Every action should move you closer to your goal. Instead of hoping you will achieve your goal—expect success.

Manipulating Your Thoughts to Focus on Success

There are three easy things you can do to control your thoughts and direct them on a path to success.

1. Focus on what you want, not on what you'll need to stop doing or start doing to get what you want. If you want to lose weight, visualize yourself as thin and beautiful. If you want to purchase a new car, don't focus on saving the money. Keep your eyes on the prize and envision yourself driving that new car.

2. Get out the doubt. Think "WHEN" not "IF." Assume success by acting as if you already have what you want.

3. Lead without looking back. Expect others to follow your lead, because they will. When you lead with confidence and conviction, they will follow. When you lead with weakness and doubt, they will follow that as well.

The Driving Force for Success

The driving force for success is passion. If you are not passionate about your purpose, then how will you successfully manipulate others to assist in achieving your desired outcome? The thing about a great mindset is that it's highly contagious. Those who you are manipulating will mimic your mood and feelings, so make sure they are confident and powerful. Having a passion for your desired outcome is this.

P = Practicing positive self-talk

A = Assuming success

S = Set your expectations

S = Search every alternative

I = Identify your desired outcome

O = Offer the best solution to others

N = Nothing can stop you from getting what you want!

When you are passionate about what you want, you naturally talk excitedly about it, and your enthusiasm attracts others to your cause. Those you can most easily manipulate may not be the first to join in; past people who practiced harmful manipulation on them made them wary of your intentions. You might have to reach out to them a little more. However, once your passion has spread, they'll be your most loyal champions. They continue to spread the word, like little ambassadors of your ideas. The nurturing and reassuring may take more energy, but it will be well worth it.

Without even realizing it, you'll soon be practicing NLP. Your thoughts and focus will change, your language will change, and you'll be able to use past programming to mold your future and that of those you are manipulating. Sound manipulation is when everybody wins!

Conclusion

Thank you for purchasing *Manipulation: The Complete Step-by-Step Guide on Manipulation, Mind Control, and NLP*.

I hope this book will help you to get what you want by applying our step-by-step strategies on achieving your desired outcome through positive manipulation. Success isn't always immediate, but as you learn the art of positive focus and develop single-minded determination to get what you want, others will be attracted to your success. Using the five steps presenting in this book will help you manipulate the beliefs and behaviors of others, and change their reality right along with yours.

The next step is to practice our step-by-step guide to successful manipulations. When you master these steps, you can achieve success in your personal relationships, career goals, and attain those material things you've always dreamed of owning. To manipulate successfully, you need to focus and be passionate about your goals. People will follow your lead, whether you are confident and excited or weak and doubtful. How you manipulate is as important as who you manipulate.

Finally, if you enjoyed this book, you'll want to read some of my other works, such as *Manipulation: The Definitive Guide to Understanding Manipulation, Mind Control, and NLP*, and *Manipulation Mastery: How to Master Manipulation, Mind Control, and NLP*. You'll gain even more insight into the wonders of manipulating others to get them to help you achieve success. Making sure everybody wins is paramount to sustained success in your manipulations.

Thank you and good luck on all your future manipulations!

Thank you!

Before you go, I just wanted to say thank you for purchasing my book.

You could have picked from dozens of other books on the same topic but you took a chance and chose this one.

So, a HUGE thanks to you for getting this book and for reading all the way to the end.

Now I wanted to ask you for a small favor. **Could you please take just a few minutes to leave a review for this book on Amazon?**

This feedback will help us continue to write the type of books that will help you get the results you want. So if you loved it, please let us know! (-:

www.ingramcontent.com/pod-product-compliance
Lightning Source LLC
Chambersburg PA
CBHW080214040426
42333CB00044B/2672